IN SPANISH PRISONS

In Spanish Prisons

THE INQUISITION AT HOME AND ABROAD
PRISONS PAST AND PRESENT

by

MAJOR ARTHUR GRIFFITHS
Late Inspector of Prisons in Great Britain

Author of
" The Mysteries of Police and Crime
" Fifty Years of Public Service," etc.

DORSET PRESS
New York

This edition published by Dorset Press,
a division of Marboro Books Corporation.
1991 Dorset Press

ISBN 0-88029-683-6

Printed in t'
M 9

INTRODUCTION

A CONSIDERABLE portion of this volume is devoted to the Spanish Inquisition, which was, for three centuries, the most important force in Spain. Thousands were condemned by its tribunals, and its prisons and punishments make up a large part of the penal history of that country. Much exaggeration has crept into the popular accounts, but the simple truth must cause a shudder, when read to-day.

The institution was created to deal with heresy, that is, with a departure from the accepted canons. The idea that there can be unity in diversity was not understood. The spiritual and the temporal powers were closely related, and bishop and king, pope and emperor, all believed that uniformity was necessary. Hence, heresy was everywhere treated as high treason not only to the Church but to the State as well. The Spanish Inquisition was a state affair as well as an ecclesiastical court.

We shall see that the jurisdiction of the Inquisition was not confined to the suppression of heresy. Many crimes which to-day are purely state concerns, were then punished by it, including bigamy, blasphemy, perjury, unnatural crimes, and witchcraft.

The Spanish Inquisition deserves credit for discouraging persecution of the last named offence, and thereby saved the lives of thousands, who, in any other state would have been executed.

The adaptation to penal purposes of ancient buildings, to be found throughout the length and breadth of Spain, was very common, as these were immediately available although generally unsuitable. Chief among them are the many monastic buildings vacated when the laws broke up religious houses in Spain and which were mostly converted into prisons, but little deserving the name. Some of these houses have been utilised as gaols pure and simple; some have served two or more purposes as at Huelva, where the convent-prison was also a barrack.

Spain has been slow in conforming to the movements towards prison reform. She could not afford to spend money on new constructions along modern lines, and the introduction of the cellular system is only of recent date. The model prison of Madrid, which has replaced the hideous Saladero, was only begun in 1887. But a few separate prisons had already been created, such as those of Loja, Pontevedra, Barcelona, Vittoria and Naval Carnero. These establishments are new to Spain but their methods and aims are too well known to call for fresh description. More interest attaches to the older forms that have so long served as places of durance.

CONTENTS

IN SPANISH PRISONS

CHAPTER I

THE INQUISITION IN SPAIN

Beginning and growth of religious persecution — Temporal power of the Papacy — Pope Innocent III creates the first "Inquisitors" — Domingo de Guzman founder of the Inquisition — Founder of the Dominican Order of Friars — The "ancient" Inquisition — Penances inflicted — Persecution of the Jews in Spain — Institution of the "modern" Inquisition under Ferdinand and Isabella — Headquarters at Seville — Frequent *autos da fé* — Thomas de Torquemada the first Inquisitor-General — The privileges of the office — Torquemada's life and character — Sufferings of accused persons.

THE record of religious persecution furnishes some of the saddest pages in the world's history. It began with the immediate successors of Constantine the Great, the first Christian prince. They promulgated severe edicts against heretics with such penalties as confiscation, banishment and death against breaches of Catholic unity. In this present tolerant age when every one may worship God after his own fashion, it is difficult to realise how recent a growth is toleration. For more than six centuries the flames of persecution burned fiercely throughout

Christendom, lighted by the strong arm of the law, and soldiers were constantly engaged to extirpate dissent from the accepted dogmas with fire and sword. The growth of the papacy and the assumption of the temporal power exalted heresy into treason; independence of thought was deemed opposition to authority and resistance to the universal supremacy of the Church. The popes fighting in self-defence stimulated the zeal of their followers unceasingly to stamp out heresy. Alexander III in the 12th century solemnly declared that every secular prince who spared heretics should be classed as a heretic himself and involved in the one common curse.

When the temporal power of the popes was fully established and acknowledged, the papacy claimed universal sovereignty over all countries and peoples and was in a position to enforce it by systematic procedure against its foes. Pope Innocent III, consumed with the fervour of his intolerant faith, determined to crush heresy. His first step was to appoint two " inquisitors " (the first use of the name) and two learned and devout friars, who were really travelling commissioners, were sent to perambulate Christendom to discover heresy. They were commended to all bishops, who were strictly charged to receive them with kindness, treat them with affection, and " help them to turn heretics from the error of their way or else drive them out of the country." The same assistance was expected from the rulers of states who were to aid the inquisitors with equal kindness.

The mission began in the south of France and a crusade was undertaken against the Albigensians and Waldensians, those early dissidents from the Church of Rome, who drew down on themselves the unappeasable animosity of the orthodox. The campaign against these original heretics raged fiercely, but persecution slackened and might have died out but for the appearance of one devoted zealot whose intense hatred of heresy, backed by his uncompromising energy, revived the illiberal spirit and organised fresh methods of attack. This was Domingo de Guzman, a Spanish monk who accompanied Foulques, Bishop of Toulouse, when he left his desolated diocese to take part in the fourth Lateran Council, assembled at Rome in 1215. This Domingo, historically known as St. Dominic, was the founder of the Dominican order of friars.

Though generally accepted as such by Church historians, it is now argued that St. Dominic was not really the founder of the Inquisition [1] and that although he spent the best years of his life in combating heresy he took no more prominent part in persecution than hundreds of others. His eulogistic biographer describes him as " a man of earnest, resolute purpose, of deep and unalterable convictions, full of burning zeal for the propagation of the faith, yet kindly in heart, cheerful in temper and

[1] Lea. History of the Inquisition. Vol. I. p. 299.

winning in manner. . . . He was as severe with himself as with his fellows. . . . His endless scourgings, his tireless vigils, his almost uninterrupted prayer, his superhuman fasts, are probably only harmless exaggerations of the truth." The Dominicans boasted that their founder exhaled " an odour of sanctity " and, when his tomb was opened, a delicious scent issued forth, so penetrating that it permeated the whole land, and so persistent that those who touched the holy relics had their hands perfumed for years.

Whatever the personal character of Dominic and whether or no he laboured to carry out the work himself, there can be no doubt that his Order was closely identified with the Inquisition from the first. Its members were appointed inquisitors, they served in the prisons as confessors, they assisted the tribunals as " qualificators," or persons appointed to seek out proof of guilt, or estimate the extent or quality of the heretical opinions charged against the accused; the great ceremonials and *autos da fé* were organised by them; they worked the " censure " and prepared the " Index " of prohibited books. The Dominicans were undoubtedly the most active agents in the Inquisition and they owed their existence to him, even if he did not personally take part in its proceedings.

The following quotation from Prescott's " History of Ferdinand and Isabella " may well be inserted here. " Some Catholic writers would fain excuse St. Dominic from the imputation of having founded the Inquisition. It is true he died some years before the perfect organisation of that tribunal; but as he established the principles on which, and the monkish militia by whom it was administered, it is doing him no injustice to regard him as its real author." The Sicilian writer, Paramo, indeed, in his heavy quarto, traces it up to a much more remote antiquity. According to him God was the first inquisitor and his condemnation of Adam and Eve furnished the models of the judicial forms observed in the trials of the Holy Office. The sentence of Adam was the type of the Inquisitional " reconciliation," his subsequent raiment of skins of animals was the type of the *sanbenito,* and the expulsion from Paradise, the precedent for the confiscation of the goods of heretics. This learned personage deduces a succession of inquisitors through the patriarchs, Moses, Nebuchadnezzar, and King David, down to John the Baptist, and he even includes our Saviour in whose precepts and conduct he finds abundant authority for the tribunal.

The " Ancient Inquisition," as that first established in Spain is generally called, had many of the features of the " modern " which dates from the reign of Ferdinand and Isabella, and which will presently be described at some length. Its proceedings were shrouded in the same impenetrable secrecy, it used the same insidious modes of accusation, supported them by similar tortures, and punished them with similar penalties. A manual drawn up in the fourteenth century for the guidance of judges of the Holy Office prescribes the familiar forms of artful interrogation employed to catch the unwary, and sometimes innocent victim. The ancient Inquisition worked on principles less repugnant to justice than the better known, but equally cruel modern institution, but was less extensive in its operations because in the earlier days there were fewer heretics to persecute.

The ancient Inquisition was so unsparing in its actions that it almost extirpated the Albigensian heresy. The punishments it inflicted were even more severe than in the modern. Upon such as escaped the stake and were " reconciled," as it was styled, a terrible " penance " was imposed. One is cited by Llorente [1] as laid down in the ordinances of St. Dominic. The penitent, it was commanded, should be stripped of his clothes and beaten by a priest three Sundays in succession from the gate of the city to the door of the church; he must not eat any kind of meat during his whole life; must abstain from fish, oil and wine three days in the week during life, except in case of sickness or excessive labour; must wear a religious dress with a small cross embroidered on each breast; must attend mass every day, if he has the means of doing so, and vespers on Sundays and festivals; must recite the service for the day and night and repeat the pater-

[1] History of the Inquisition.

noster seven times in the day, ten times in the evening, and twenty times at midnight. If he failed in any of these requirements, he was to be burned as a "relapsed heretic."

Chief among the causes that produced the new or "modern" Inquisition was the envy and hatred of the Jews in Spain. Fresh material was supplied by the unfortunate race of Israel, long established in the country, and greatly prosperous. They had come in great numbers after the Saracenic invasion, which indeed they are said to have facilitated, and were accepted by some of the Moorish rulers on nearly equal terms, and were treated with a tolerance seldom seen among Mahometans, though occasional outbursts of fanaticism rendered their position not quite secure. Under these generally favourable auspices the Jews developed in numbers and importance. Their remarkable instinct for money making and their unstinting diligence brought them great wealth. Their love of letters and high intelligence gave them preëminence in the schools of the Moorish cities of Cordova, Toledo and Granada, where they helped to keep the flame of learning bright and shining through the darkest ages. They became noted mathematicians, learned astronomers, devoted labourers in the fields of practical and experimental science. Their shrewdness in public affairs and their financial abilities commended them to the service of the state, and many rose to the highest civic dignities at both Christian and Moorish courts. Often, despite prohibitory laws, they collected the revenues and supervised the treasuries of the kingdoms of Castile and Aragon, while in private life they had nearly unlimited control of commerce and owned most of the capital in use.

After the Christian conquest, their success drew down upon them the envy and hatred of their less flourishing fellow subjects, who resented also that profuse ostentation of apparel and equipage to which the Jewish character has always inclined. Their widespread practice of usury was a still more fruitful cause for detestation. Often large sums were loaned, for which exorbitant rates of interest were charged, owing to the scarcity of specie and the great risk of loss inherent to the business. As much as twenty, thirty-three, and even forty per cent. per annum was exacted and paid. The general animosity was such that a fanatical populace, smarting under a sense of wrong, and urged on by a no less fanatical clergy broke out at times into violence, and fiercely attacked the Jews in the principal cities. The *Juderías*, or Jewish quarters, were sacked, the houses robbed of their valuable contents, precious collections, jewels and furniture were scattered abroad, and the wretched proprietors were massacred wholesale, irrespective of sex and age. According to the historian, Mariana, fifty thousand Jews were sacrificed to the popular fury in one year, 1391, alone.

This was the turning point in Spanish history. Fanaticism once aroused, did not die until all Jews were driven out of Spain. It brought into being another class also, the *Conversos,* or " New Christians," *i. e.* Jews who accepted Christian baptism, though generally without any spiritual change. At heart and in habits they remained Jews.

The law was invoked, too, to aggravate their condition. Legislative enactments of a cruel and oppressive kind were passed. Jews were forbidden to mix freely with Christians, their residence restricted to certain limited quarters, they were subject to irksome, sumptuary regulations, debarred from all display in dress, forbidden to carry valuable ornaments or wear expensive clothes, and they were held up to public scorn by being compelled to appear in a distinctive, unbecoming garb, the badge or emblem of their social inferiority. They were also interdicted from following certain professions and callings. They might not study or practise medicine, might not be apothecaries, nurses, vintners, grocers or tavern keepers, were forbidden to act as stewards to the nobility or as farmers or collectors of the public revenues, although judging from repeated reenactments, these laws were evidently not strictly enforced, and often in some districts were not enforced at all.

Fresh fuel was added to the fiery passions vented on the Jews by the unceasing denunciation of their heresy and dangerous irreligion, and public feeling was further inflamed by grossly exaggerated stories of their hideous and unchristian malpractices. The curate of Los Palacios has detailed some of these in his " Chronicle," and they will serve, when quoted, to show what charges were brought against the Jew in his time. " This accursed race (the Israelites)," he says, speaking of the proceedings taken to bring about their conversion, " were either unwilling to bring their children to be baptised, or if they did, they washed away the stain on the way home. They dressed their stews and other dishes with oil instead of lard, abstained from pork, kept the passover, ate meat in Lent, and sent oil to replenish the lamps of their synagogues, with many other abominable cere- monies of their religion. They entertained no re- spect for monastic life, and frequently profaned the sanctity of religious houses by the violation or se- duction of their inmates. They were an exceedingly politic and ambitious people, engrossing the most lucrative municipal offices, and preferring to gain their livelihood by traffic, in which they made exor- bitant gains, rather than by manual labour or me- chanical arts. They considered themselves in the hands of the Egyptians whom it was a merit to de- ceive and rob. By their wicked contrivances they amassed great wealth, and thus were able often to ally themselves by marriage with noble Christian families."

The outcry against the Jews steadily increased in volume. The clergy were the loudest in their protests against the alleged abominations, and one Dominican priest, Alonso de Hojeda, prior of the monastery of San Pablo in Seville, with another priest, Diego de Merlo, vigorously denounced the " Jewish leprosy " so alarmingly on the increase and besought the Catholic sovereigns to revive the Holy Office with extended powers as the only effective means of healing it. The appeal was strongly supported by the papal nuncio at the Court of Castile. Ferdinand and Isabella, as devout Catholics, deplored the prevalence of heresy, which they acknowledged to be rampant, and yet they hesitated to surrender any of their independence. No other state in Europe was so free from papal control or interference. Some of the Conversos held high places about the court and they, of course, used every effort to strengthen the reluctance of the queen, particularly. On the other hand, the Dominican monk, Thomas de Torquemada, her confessor in her youth, strove to instil the same spirit of unyielding fanaticism that possessed himself, and earnestly entreated her to devote herself to the " extirpation of heresy for the glory of God and the glorification of the Catholic faith." She long resisted but yielded at last to the unceasing importunities of the priests around her, and consented to solicit a bull from the pope, Sixtus IV, to introduce the Modern Inquisition into Castile. It was issued, under the date of November 1st, 1478, and authorised the appointment of two or three ecclesiastical inquisitors for the detection and suppression of heresy throughout Spain.

One difference from the usual form establishing such tribunals was the location of the power of appointment of inquisitors, which was vested in the king and queen instead of in Provincials of the Dominican or Franciscan Orders. Heretofore the appointment of inquisitors had been considered a delegation of the authority of the Holy See, something entirely independent of the secular power. But so jealous of outside interference were the Spanish rulers and the Spanish people, that the pope was forced to give way. Though he and his successors vainly strove to recover the power thus granted, they were never entirely successful, and the Spanish Inquisition remained to a large extent a state affair, and this fact explains much which otherwise is inexplicable. For example the confiscations passed into the royal instead of into the papal treasury.

At first mild measures were to be tried. Cardinal Mendoza, Archbishop of Seville, had drawn up a catechism instructing his clergy to spare no pains in illuminating the benighted Israelites by a candid exposition of the true principles of Christianity. Progress was slow, and after two years the results were so meagre that it was thought necessary to proceed to the nomination of inquisitors, and two Dominican monks, Fra Miguel de Morillo, and Juan de San Martin, were appointed with full powers, assisted by an assessor and a procurator fiscal.

The Jews played into the hands of their tormentors. Great numbers had been terrified into apostasy by the unrelenting hostility of the people. Their only escape from the furious attacks made upon them had been conversion to Christianity, often quite feigned and unreal. The proselytising priests, however, claimed to have done wonders; one, St. Vincent Ferrer, a Dominican of Valencia, had by means of his eloquence and the miraculous power vouchsafed him, " changed the hearts of no less than thirty-five thousand of house of Judah." These numerous converts were of course unlikely to be very tenacious in their profession of the new faith, and not strangely laid themselves open to constant suspicion. Many were denounced and charged with backsliding, many more boldly reverted to Judaism, or secretly performed their old rites. Now uncompromising war was to be waged against the backsliding " new Christians " or Conversos.

The inquisitors installed themselves in Seville, and made the Dominican convent of San Pablo their first headquarters, but this soon proved quite insufficient in size and they were allowed to occupy the fortress of the Triana, the great fortress of Seville, on the right bank of the Guadalquivir, the immense size and gloomy dungeons of which were especially suitable. This part of the city was much

exposed to inundations, and when, in 1626, it was
threatened with destruction by an unusually high
flood, the seat of the tribunal was removed to the
palace of the Caballeros Tellos Taveros in the parish
of San Marco. In 1639 it returned to the Triana
which had been repaired, and remained there till
1789, when further encroachments of the river
caused it to be finally transferred to the College of
Las Beccas. The Triana is now a low suburb, in-
habited principally by gipsies and the lower classes.
It was at one time the potters' quarter where the
famous *azulejo* tiles were made, and its factories
to-day produce the well known majolica vases and
plates with surface of metallic lustre.

One of the first steps of the Inquisition was to put
a summary check to the exodus of the Jews who had
been fast deserting the country. All the magnates
of Castile, dukes, counts, hidalgos and persons in
authority, were commanded to arrest all fugitives,
to sequestrate their property and send them prisoners to Seville. Any who disobeyed or failed to exe-
cute this order were to be excommunicated as abettors of heresy, to be deposed from their dignities
and deprived of their estates. Such orders were
strange to the ears of the turbulent nobles who had
been accustomed to pay little heed to pope or king.
A new force had arisen in the land.

On the Castle of the Triana,[1] already described, a

[1] The counts of San Lucar were hereditary alcaldes of
Triana, and in return for surrendering the castle, they were

tablet was erected over the portals with an inscription, celebrating the inauguration of the first " modern Inquisition " in Western Europe. The concluding words were : — " God grant that for the protection and augmentation of the faith it may abide unto the end of time. Arise oh Lord, judge Thy cause! Catch yet the foxes (heretics)!"

Just now, by an ill-advised move, the Conversos lost the sympathy of all. Diego de Susan, one of the richest citizens of Seville, called a meeting of the " New Christians " in the church of San Salvador. It was attended by many high officials, and even ecclesiastics of Jewish blood. Susan suggested that they collect a store of arms, and that at the first arrest, they rise and slay the inquisitors. The plan was adopted but was betrayed by a daughter of Susan, who had a Christian lover. The plotters were arrested at once, and on February sixth, 1481, six men and women were burned and others were severely punished.

The hunt was cunningly organised. An " Edict of Grace " was published promising pardon to all backsliders if they would come voluntarily and confess their sins. Many sought indulgence and were plied with questions by the inquisitors to extract evidence against others. On the information thus

granted the dignity of Alguazil Mayor of the Inquisition. It was worth 150,000 maravedis a year and the holder of the office provided a deputy. The maravedi, once a gold coin of some value, latterly represented only $\frac{3}{8}$ of a cent.

obtained the suspected were marked down, seized and carried off to the prisons. Any adherence to Jewish customs gave opportunity for denunciation, and the severe measures rapidly reduced the numbers of the backsliding Jewish-Christians. In Seville alone, according to Llorente, two hundred and ninety-eight persons were burnt in less than a year, and seventy-nine were condemned to perpetual imprisonment. Great sums ought to have passed into the treasury, then and afterwards, from the confiscated property of rich people who perished at the stake or were subjected to fine and forfeiture. But the great engine of the Inquisition was excessively costly. The pageants at the frequent *autos da fé* were lavishly expensive, a great staff of officials, experts, familiars and guards was maintained, and, in addition, the outlay on the place of execution, the " *quemadero* " or burning place, a great pavement on a raised platform adorned with fine pillars and statues of the prophets, was very considerable, while the yearly bill for fuel, for faggots and brush wood rose to a high figure. Undoubtedly there was considerable embezzlement also.

There was evidently too much work for two men, so in February, 1482, seven additional inquisitors were commissioned by the pope on the nomination of the sovereigns, and some of these were exceedingly zealous. There was, however, much confusion because of the lack of a unifying authority. The sovereigns were determined that the institution must be kept under the control of the state, and so a council of administration usually called *la Suprema* was added to those already existing, and was charged with jurisdiction over all measures concerning the faith. At the head was placed a new officer, later called the inquisitor-general. The inquisitor-general was hardly a subject. He had direct access to the sovereign and exercised absolute and unlimited power over the whole population and was superior to all human law. No rank, high or low escaped his jurisdiction. Royal personages were not exempt from his control, for the Holy Office invaded the prince's palace as well as the pauper's hovel. There was no sanctity in the grave, for corpses of heretics were ruthlessly disinterred, mutilated and burned.

The first inquisitor-general under the new organisation was Thomas de Torquemada, who has won for himself dreadful immortality from the signal part he played in the great tragedy of the Inquisition. He was a Dominican monk, a native of old Castile, who had been confessor and keeper of the Queen's conscience to Isabella in her early days and constantly sought to instil his fiery spirit into her youthful mind. "This man," says Prescott, "who concealed more pride under his monastic weeds than might have furnished forth a convent of his order, was one of that class with whom zeal passes for religion and who testify their zeal by a fiery persecution of those whose creed differs from their

own; who compensate for their abstinence from
sensual indulgence by giving scope to those deadlier
vices of the heart, pride, bigotry and intolerance
which are no less opposed to virtue and are far more
extensively mischievous to society." The cruelties
which he perpetrated grew out of a pitiless fanaticism, more cruel than the grave. He was rigid and
unbending and knew no compromise. Absolutely
fearless, he directed his terrible engine against the
suspect no matter how high-born or influential.

Torquemada was appointed in 1483 and was authorised from Rome to frame a new constitution
for the Holy Office. He had been empowered to
create permanent provincial tribunals under chief
inquisitors which sat at Toledo, Valladolid, Madrid
and other important cities, and his first act was to
summon some of these to Seville to assist him in
drawing up rules for the governance of the great
and terrible engine that was to terrorise all Spain
for centuries to come. The principles of action, the
methods of procedure, the steps taken to hunt up
victims and bring them under the jurisdiction of
the court, secure conviction and enforce penalties,
are all set out at length in the record of the times.
" A bloody page of history," says the historian,
" attests the fact that fanaticism armed with power
is the sorest evil that can befall a nation." For
generations the Spanish people, first the Jews, then
the Moriscos, lastly the whole native born com-
munity lay helpless in the grip of this irresponsible

despotism. Few, once accused, escaped without censure of some sort. Llorente declares with his usual exaggeration that out of a couple of thousand cases, hardly one ended in acquittal and the saying became proverbial that people if not actually roasted by the Inquisition were at least singed.

In order to appreciate fully the harshness of the Spanish Inquisition and the cruelties perpetrated for several centuries, under the guise of religion, we must trace the steps taken by the Holy Office, its guiding principles and its methods of procedure.

The great aim at the outset was to hunt up heretics and encourage the denunciation of presumed offenders. Good Catholics were commanded by edicts published from the pulpits of all churches to give information against every person they knew or suspected of being guilty of heresy, and priests were ordered to withhold absolution from any one who hesitated to speak, even when the suspected person was a near relation, parent, child, husband or wife. All accusations whether signed or anonymous were accepted, but the names of witnesses were also required. On this sometimes meagre inculpation victims might be at once arrested, though in some cases, censors must first pass upon the evidence. Often not a whisper of trouble reached the accused until the blow actually fell.

Kept thus in solitary imprisonment, cut off entirely from his friends outside, denied the sympathy or support he might derive from their visits or communications, he was left to brood despairingly, a prey to agonised doubts, in ignorance even of the charges brought against him. A few brief extracts from the depositions of witnesses might be read to him, but the statements were so garbled that he could get no clue to names or identities. If there were any facts favourable to him in the testimony they were withheld from him. If he could, however, name as mortal enemies some of the witnesses, their testimony was much weakened. Facts of time, place and circumstance in the charges preferred were withheld from him and he was so confused and embarrassed that unless a man of acuteness and presence of mind he might become involved in inextricable contradictions when he attempted to explain himself.

On the other hand judges were guided and supported by the most minute instructions. " It is the high and peculiar privilege of the tribunal that its officers are not required to act with formality; they need observe no strict forensic rules and therefore the omission of what ordinary justice might exact does not invalidate its actions, provided only that nothing essential to the proof be wanting." The first essential of justice, as we understand it, was ignored. An accused person arraigned for heresy was expected to incriminate himself, to furnish all necessary particulars for conviction. Testimony could be received from persons of any class or character. " They might be excommunicate, infamous, actual accomplices, or previously convicted of any crime." The evidence of Jews and infidels might be taken also, even in a question of heretical doctrine. Wife, children, relatives, servants, might depose against a heretic. "A brother may declare against a brother and a son against a father." The witnesses met with no mercy. If any one did not say all he could, or seemed reluctant to speak, the examiners occasionally ruled that torture should be applied.

CHAPTER II

PERSECUTION OF JEWS AND MOORS

Increased persecution of the Jews — Accusations made against them — Ferdinand introduces the modern Inquisition into the Kingdom of Aragon in 1484 — Fray Gaspar Juglar and Pedro Arbués appointed Inquisitors — Assassination of Pedro Arbués — Punishment of his murderers — Increased opposition against the Holy Office — Arrest of the Infante Don Jaime for sheltering a heretic — Expulsion of the Jews from Spain — Appeal to the King to revoke this edict — Ferdinand inclined to yield, but Torquemada over-rules him — Sufferings of the Jews on the journey — Death of Torquemada — Hernando de Talavera appointed archbishop of Granada — His success with the Moors — Don Diego Deza new Inquisitor-General — Succeeded by Ximenes de Cisneros — His character and life — Appointed Primate of all Spain — His severity with the Moors — University of Alcalá founded by Ximenes — Accession of Charles V — Persecution of Moors — Expulsion.

THE fires of the modern Inquisition, it was said, had been lighted exclusively for the Jews. The fiery zeal of Torquemada and his coadjutors was first directed against the Spanish children of Israel. The Jews constantly offered themselves to be harassed and despoiled. They were always fair game for avaricious greed. The inquisitors availed themselves of both lines of attack. Jewish wealth steadily increased as their financial operations and their industrial activities extended and flourished. When the Catholic Kings embarked upon the conquest of Granada, the Jews found the sinews of war; Jewish victuallers purveyed rations to the armies in the field; Jewish brokers advanced the cash needed for the payments of troops; Jewish armourers repaired the weapons used and furnished new tools and warlike implements.

At the same time the passions of the populace were more and more inflamed against the Jews by the dissemination of scandalous stories of their blasphemous proceedings. It was seriously asserted by certain monks that some Jews had stolen a consecrated wafer with the intention of working it into a paste with the warm blood of a newly killed Christian child and so produce a deadly poison to be administered to the hated chief inquisitor. Another report was to the effect that crumbs from the holy wafer had been detected between the leaves of a Hebrew prayer book in a synagogue. One witness declared that this substance emitted a bright effulgence which gave clear proof of its sanctity and betrayed the act of sacrilege committed. Other tales were circulated of the diabolical practices of these wicked Jewish heretics.

Ferdinand in 1484 proceeded to give the modern Inquisition to the Kingdom of Aragon, where the " ancient " had once existed but had lost much of its rigour. It was a comparatively free country and the Holy Office had become little more than an ordinary ecclesiastical court. But King Ferdinand was resolved to reëstablish it on the wider basis it had assumed in Castile and imposed it upon his people by a royal order which directed all consti-tuted authorities to support it in carrying out its new extended functions. A Dominican monk, Fray Gaspar Juglar, and a canon of the church, Pedro Arbués, were appointed by Torquemada to be in-quisitors for the diocese of Saragossa. The new institution was most distasteful to the Aragonese, a hardy and independent people. Among the higher orders were numbers of Jewish descent, filling im-portant offices and likely to come under the ban of the Inquisition. The result was a deputation to the pope and another to the king representing the gen-eral repugnance of the Aragonese to the institution and praying that its action might be suspended. Neither pope nor king would listen to the appeal and the Holy Office began its work. Two *autos da fé* were celebrated in Saragossa, the capital, in 1484, when two men were executed.

Horror and consternation seized the Conversos and a fierce desire for reprisals developed. They were resolved to intimidate their oppressors by some appalling act of retaliation and a plot was hatched to make away with one of the inquisitors. The conspirators included many of the principal " New Christians," some of whom were persons of note in the district. A considerable sum was subscribed to meet expenses and pay the assassins. Pedro Arbués was marked down for destruction but, conscious of his danger, continually managed to evade his enemies. He wore always a coat of mail beneath his robes when he attended mass in the Cathedral, and every avenue by which he could be approached in his house was also carefully guarded.

At length he was taken by surprise when at his devotions. He was on his knees before the high altar saying his prayers at midnight, when two men crept up behind him unobserved and attacked him. One struck him with a dagger in the left arm, the other felled him with a violent blow on the back of the neck by which he was laid prostrate and carried off dying. With his last breath he thanked God for being selected to seal so good a cause with his blood. His death was deemed a martyrdom and caused a reaction in favour of the Inquisition as a general rising of the New Christians was feared. The storm was appeased by the archbishop of Saragossa who gave out publicly that the murderers should be rigorously pursued and should suffer condign punishment. The promise was abundantly fulfilled. A stern recompense was exacted from all who were identified with the conspiracy. The scent was followed up with unrelenting pertinacity, several persons were taken and put to death, and a larger number perished in the dungeons of the Inquisition. All the perpetrators of the murder were hanged after their right hands had been amputated. The sentence of one who had given evidence against the rest was commuted in that his hand was not cut off till after his death.

A native of Saragossa had taken refuge in Tudela where he found shelter and concealment in the house of the Infante, Don Jaime, the illegitimate son of the Queen of Navarre, and nephew of King Ferdinand himself. The generous young prince could not reject the claims of hospitality and helped the fugitive to escape into France. But the Infante was himself arrested by the inquisitors and imprisoned as an " impeder " of the Holy Office. His trial took place in Saragossa, although Navarre was outside its jurisdiction, and he was sentenced to do open penance in the cathedral in the presence of a great congregation at High Mass. The ceremony was carried out before the Archbishop of Saragossa, a boy of seventeen, the illegitimate son of King Ferdinand, and this callow stripling in his primate's robes ordered his father's nephew to be flogged round the church with rods.

The second story is much more horrible. One Gaspar de Santa Cruz of Saragossa had been concerned in the rebellion, but escaped to Toulouse where he died. He had been aided in his flight by a son who remained in Saragossa, and who was arrested as an " impeder " of the Holy Office. He was tried and condemned to appear at an *auto da fé,* where he was made to read an act which held up his father to public ignominy. Then the son was transferred to the custody of the inquisitor of Toulouse who took him to his father's grave, forced him to exhume the corpse and burn it with his own hands.

The bitter hatred of the Jews culminated in the determination of the king and queen, urged on by Torquemada, to expel them entirely from Spain. The germ of this idea may be found in the capitulation of Granada by the Moors, when it was agreed that every Jew found in the city was to be shipped off forthwith to Barbary. It was now argued that since all attempts to convert them had failed, Spain should be altogether rid of them. The Catholic King and Queen were induced to sign an edict dated March 30th, 1492, by which it was decreed that every Jew should be banished from Spain within three months, save and except those who chose to apostasise and who, on surrendering the faith of their fathers, might be suffered to remain in the land of their adoption, with leave to enjoy the goods they had inherited or earned. No doubt this edict originated with Torquemada.

Dismay and deep sorrow fell upon the Spanish Jews. The whole country was filled with tribulation. All alike cried for mercy and offered to submit to any laws and ordinances however oppressive, to accept any terms, to pay any penalties if only they might escape this cruel exile. Leading Jews appeared before King Ferdinand and pleaded abjectly for mercy for their co-religionists, offering an immediate ransom of six hundred thousand crowns in

gold.   The king was inclined to clemency, but the
queen was firm.   He saw the present advantage, the
ready money, and doubted whether he would get
as much from the fines and confiscations promised
by the inquisitors.   But at that moment, so the story
goes, Torquemada rushed into the presence bearing
a crucifix on high and cried in stentorian tones that
the sovereigns were about to act the part of Judas
Iscariot.   " Here he is!   Sell Him again, not for
thirty pieces of silver, but for thirty thousand! " and
flinging the crucifix on to the table, he ran out in
a frenzy.   This turned the tables, and the decree for
expulsion was confirmed.

The terms of the edict were extremely harsh and
peremptory.   As a preamble the crimes of the Jews
were recited and the small effect produced hitherto
by the most severe penalties.   It was asserted that
they still conspired to overturn Christianity in Spain
and recourse to the last remedy, the decree of expulsion, under which all Jews and Jewesses were commanded to leave Spain and never return, even for
a passing visit, on pain of death, was therefore necessary.   The last day of July, 1492, or four months
later, was fixed for the last day of their sojourn in
Spain.   After that date they would remain at the
peril of their lives, while any person of whatever
rank or quality who should presume to receive, shelter, protect or defend a Jew or Jewess should for-
feit all his property and be discharged from his
office, dignity or calling.   During the four months,

the law allowed the Jews to sell their estates, or barter them for heavy goods, but they were forbidden to remove gold or silver or take out of the kingdom other portable property which was already prohibited by law from exportation.

During the preparation for, and execution of this modern exodus, the condition of the wretched Israelites was heart-rending. Torquemada had tried hard to proselytise, had sent out preachers offering baptism and reconciliation, but at first few listened to the terms proposed. All owners of property and valuables suffered the heaviest losses. Enforced sales were so numerous that purchasers were not to be easily found. Fine estates were sold for a song. A house was exchanged for an ass or beast of burden; a vineyard for a scrap of cloth or linen. Despite the prohibition much gold and silver were carried away concealed in the stuffing of saddles and among horse furniture. Some exiles at the moment of departure swallowed gold pieces, as many as twenty and thirty, and thus evaded to some extent the strict search instituted at the sea ports and frontier towns.

At last in the first week of July, all took to the roads travelling to the coast on foot, on horse or ass-back or were conveyed in country carts. According to an eye-witness, " they suffered incredible misfortunes by the way, some walking feebly, some struggling manfully, some fainting, many attacked with illness, some dying, others coming

into the world, so that there was not a Christian who
did not feel for them and entreat them to be baptised." Here and there under the pressure of accumulated miseries a few professed to be converted,
but such cases were very rare. The rabbis encouraged the people as they went and exhorted the young
ones to raise their voices and the women to sing
and play on pipes and timbrels to enliven them and
keep up their spirits.

Ships were provided by the Spanish authorities
at Cadiz, Gibraltar, Carthagena, Valencia and Barcelona on which fifteen hundred of the wealthy
families embarked and started for Africa, Italy and
the Levant, taking with them their dialect of the
Spanish language, such as is still talked at the places
where they landed. Of those who joined in the
general exodus some perished at sea, by wreck, disease, violence or fire, and some by famine, exhaus-
tion or murder on inhospitable shores. Many were
sold for slaves, many thrown overboard by savage
ship captains, while parents parted with their children for money to buy food. On board one crowded
ship a pestilence broke out, and the whole company
was landed and marooned on a desert island. Other
infected ships carried disease into the port of Na-
ples, where it grew into a terrible epidemic, by which
twenty thousand native Neapolitans perished.
Those who reached the city found it in the throes
of famine, but were met in landing by a procession
of priests, led by one who carried a crucifix and a

loaf of bread, and who intimated that only those who would adore the first would receive the other. In papal dominions alone was a hospitable reception accorded. The pope of the time, Alexander VI, was more tolerant than other rulers.

The total loss of population is now difficult to ascertain, but undoubtedly it has been greatly exaggerated. The most trustworthy estimate fixes the number of emigrants at one hundred and sixty-five thousand, and the number dying of hardships and grief before leaving at about twenty thousand. Probably fifty thousand more accepted baptism as a consequence of the edict. The loss entailed in actual value was incalculable and a vast amount of potential earnings was sacrificed by the disappearance of so large a part of the most industrious members of the population. The king and queen greatly impoverished Spain in purging it of Hebrew heresy. Their action however was greeted with applause by other rulers who did not go to the same lengths on account of economic considerations. They were praised because they were willing to sacrifice revenue for the sake of the faith.

Open Judaism no longer existed in Spain. There were left only the apostates, or New Christians. That many of these were Christians in name and kept the Mosaic law in every detail is undoubted. As Jews they were not subject to the Inquisition. As professing Christians, any departure from the established faith subjected them to the penalties

imposed upon heretics. In spite of the high posi-
tions which many achieved, they were objects of
suspicion, and with the increasing authority of the
Inquisition their lot grew harder.

Torquemada had been active not only against the
Jews, but against all suspected of any heresy, no
matter how influential. The odium he incurred
raised up constant accusations against him, and he
was obliged on three occasions to send an agent to
Rome to defend his character. Later his arbitrary
power was curtailed by the appointment of four coadjutors, nominally, to share the burthens of office,
but really to check his action. On the whole he may
be said to take rank among those who have been the
authors of evil to their species. "His zeal was of
such an extravagant character that it may almost
shelter itself under the name of insanity." His later
days were filled with constant dread of assassination, and when he moved to and fro his person was
protected by a formidable escort, a bodyguard of
fifty familiars of the Holy Office mounted as drag-
oons and a body of two hundred infantry soldiers.
Yet he reached a very old age and died quietly in
his bed.

Estimates of the numbers convicted and punished
during his administration differ widely. Llorente,
who is, however, much given to exaggeration, states
that eight thousand eight hundred were burned
alive, and that the total number condemned was
more than one hundred and five thousand. On the

other hand Langlois,[1] whose estimate is accepted by Vancandard, and other Catholic writers, thinks that the number put to death was about two thousand.

Death overtook him when a fresh campaign against heresy was imminent. The conquest of the Kingdom of Granada by Ferdinand and Isabella opened up a new field for the proselytising fervour of the Inquisition, which was now resolved to convert all Mahometan subjects to the Christian faith. A friar of the order of St. Jerome, Hernando de Talavera, a man of blameless life, a ripe scholar, a persuasive preacher, deeply read in sacred literature and moral philosophy, had been one of the confessors to Royalty, and had been raised to the bishopric of Avila. But he had begged to be allowed to resign it and devote himself entirely to the conversion of the Moors. The pope granted his request and appointed him archbishop of Granada with a smaller revenue than that of the diocese he left, but he was humble minded, had no craving to exhibit the pomp and display of a great prelate and devoted himself with all diligence to the duties of his new charge.

He soon won the hearts of the Moors who loved and venerated him. He proceeded with great caution, made no open show of his desire to convert them, and strictly refrained from any coercive measures, trusting rather to reason them out of their

[1] Langlois, L'Inquisition d'après des tableaux recénts (1902), quoted by Vancandard (Conway's translation, 1908).

heterodox belief. He caused a translation to be made of the Bible into Arabic, distributed it, encouraged the Moors to attend conferences, and come to him in private to listen to his arguments. Being thus busily engaged, he withdrew to a great extent from the court of Ferdinand and Isabella, who came more and more under the influence of fiery bigots, to whom the mild measures of the archbishop became profoundly displeasing. The inquisitors, with Don Diego Deza who had succeeded Torquemada, at their head, incessantly entreated the sovereigns to proceed with more severity, and went the length of advising the immediate expulsion of all Moors who hesitated to accept conversion and baptism forthwith. They urged that it was for the good of their souls to draw them into the fold and insisted that it would be utterly impossible for Christian and Moslem to live peacefully and happily side by side. The king and queen demurred, temporising as they had done with the revival of the Inquisition. It might be dangerous, they argued, to enforce penalties that were too harsh. Their supremacy was hardly as yet consolidated in Granada; the Moors had not yet entirely laid aside their arms and unwise oppression might bring about a resumption of hostilities. They hoped that the Moors, like other conquered peoples, would in due course freely adopt the religion of their new masters. Loving kindliness and gentle persuasion would more surely gain ground than fierce threats and arbitrary decrees.

So for seven or more years the conciliatory methods of Archbishop Talavera prevailed and met with the approval of Ferdinand and Isabella. But now a remarkable man of very different character appeared upon the scene and began to advocate sterner measures. This was a Franciscan monk, Ximenes de Cisneros, one of the most notable figures in Spanish history, who became in due course inquisitor-general and regent of Spain. A sketch of his life may well be given to enable us better to understand the times.

Ximenes de Cisneros better known, perhaps, under his first name alone, was the scion of an ancient but decayed family and destined from his youth for the Church. He studied at the University of Salamanca and evinced marked ability. After a stay in Rome, the best field for preferment, he returned to Spain with the papal promise of the first vacant benefice in the See of Toledo. The archbishop had other views, however, and when Ximenes claimed the cure of Uceda, he was sent to prison in its fortress and not to the presbytery. For six years Ximenes asserted his pretensions unflinchingly and was at last nominated, when he exchanged to a chaplaincy in another diocese, that of Siguenza, where he continued his theological studies and acquired Hebrew and Chaldee. Here he came under the observation of the Bishop Mendoza, who afterwards became Cardinal Primate of Spain, and who enjoyed the unbounded confidence of Queen Isabella. Mendoza when invited to recommend to her a new confessor, in succession to Talavera on his translation to the See of Granada, fixed upon Ximenes of whom he had never lost sight since their first acquaintance at Siguenza.

Ximenes, meanwhile, had become more and more devoted to his sacred calling. His marked business aptitudes had gained for him the post of steward to a great nobleman, the Conde de Cifuentes, who had been taken prisoner by the Moors. But secular concerns were distasteful to him and Ximenes resigned his charge. His naturally austere and contemplative disposition had deepened into stern fanatical enthusiasm and he resolved to devote himself more absolutely to the service of the Church. He entered the Franciscan order, threw up all his benefices and employments, and became a simple novice in the monastery of San Juan de los Reyes in Toledo, where his cloister life was signalised by extreme severity and self-mortification. He wore haircloth next his skin, slept on the stone floor with a wooden pillow under his head, tortured himself with continual fasts and vigils, and flogged himself perpetually. At last he became a professed monk, and because of the fame of his exemplary piety, great crowds were attracted to his confessional. He shrank now from the popular favour and retired to a lonely convent in a far off forest, where he built himself a small hermitage with his own hands and where he passed days and nights in solemn abstraction and unceasing prayer, living like the ancient anchorites on the green herbs he gathered and drinking water from the running streams. Self centred and pondering deeply on spiritual concerns, constantly in a state of mental exaltation and ecstasy, he saw visions and dreamed dreams, believing himself to be in close communication with celestial agencies and was no doubt on the eve of going mad, when his superiors ordered him to reside in the convent of Salceda, where he became charged with its administration and management, and was forced to exercise his powerful mind for the benefit of others.

It was here that the call to court found him and he was summoned to Valladolid and unexpectedly brought into the presence of the queen. Isabella was greatly prepossessed in his favour by his simple dignity of manner, his discretion, his unembarrassed self-possession and above all his fervent piety in discussing religious questions. Yet he hesitated to accept the office of her confessor, and only did so on the condition that he should be allowed to conform to the rules of his order and remain at his monastery except when officially on duty at the court.

Soon afterwards, he was appointed Provincial of the Franciscans in Castile and set himself to reform their religious houses, the discipline of which was greatly relaxed. Sloth, luxury and licentiousness prevailed and especially in his own order, which was wealthy and richly endowed with estates

in the country, and stately dwellings in the towns.
These monks, styled "conventuals," wasted large
sums in prodigal expenditure, and were often guilty
of scandalous misconduct which Ximenes, as an
Observantine, one of a small section pledged to rigid
observance of monastic rules, strongly condemned.
He was encouraged and supported in the work of
reform by Isabella and a special bull from Rome
armed him with full authority. His rigorous and
unsparing action met with fierce opposition, but he
triumphed in the end and won a notable reward.
When the archbishop of Toledo died, in 1495,
Ximenes, unknown to himself, was selected for the
great post of primate of all Spain and Lord High
Chancellor of Castile.

The right to nominate was vested in the Queen,
and Ferdinand in this instance begged her to appoint his natural son, Alfonso, already archbishop
of Saragossa, but a child almost in years. She
firmly and unhesitatingly refused and recommended
her confessor to the pope as the most worthy re-
cipient of the honour. When the bull making the
appointment arrived from Rome, the queen summoned Ximenes to her presence handed him the
letter and desired him to open it before her. On
reading the address, "To our venerable brother,
Francisco Ximenes de Cisneros, Archbishop of
Toledo," he changed colour, dropped the letter, and
crying, "There must be some mistake," ran out of
the room. The queen, in surprise, waited, but he

did not return and it was found that he had taken horse and fled to his monastery. Two grandees were despatched in hot haste to ride after him, overtake him and bring him back to Madrid. He returned but still resisted all the entreaties of his friends and the clearly expressed wishes of his sovereign. Finally his persistent refusal was overborne, but only by the direct command of the pope, who ordered him to accept the post for which his sovereigns had chosen him. He has been sharply criticised for his apparent humility, but it is generally admitted that he was sincere in his refusal. He was already advanced in years, ambition was dying in him, he had become habituated to monastic seclusion and his thoughts were already turned from the busy turmoil of this world to the life beyond the grave.

However reluctant to accept high office, Ximenes was by no means slow to exercise the power it gave him. He ruled the Spanish Church with a rod of iron, bending all his energies to the work of reforming the practices of the clergy, enforcing discipline and insisting upon the maintenance of the strictest morality. He trod heavily, made many enemies, and stirred so much ill feeling that the malcontents combined to despatch a messenger to lay their grievances before the pope. The officious advocate, however, got no audience but went home to Spain, where twenty months' imprisonment taught him not to offend again the masterful archbishop of Toledo.

Ximenes in insisting upon a strict observance of
propriety and the adoption of an exemplary life, was
in himself a model to the priesthood. He never relaxed the personal mortifications which had been his
rule when a simple monk. He kept no state and
made no show, regulating his domestic expenditure
with the strictest and most parsimonious economy,
until reminded by the Holy See that the dignity of
his great office demanded more magnificence. Still,
when he increased his display and the general style
of living in household, equipages and the number
of his retainers, he continued to be as harsh as ever
to himself.

In spite of all opposition and discontent he pursued his course with inflexible purpose. His spirit
was unyielding, and his energetic proceedings were
unremittingly directed to the amelioration and improvement in the morals of the clergy with marked
success. And now he set himself with the same
uncompromising zeal to extirpate heresy. Having
begged Archbishop Talavera to allow him to join in
the good work at Granada, he took immediate advantage of the consent given and began to attack the
Moorish unbelievers in his own vigorous fashion.
His first step was to call together a great conference of learned Mussulman doctors, to whom he ex-
pounded with all the eloquence he had at his command, the true doctrines of the Catholic faith and
their superiority to the law of Mahomet. He accompanied his teaching with liberal gifts, chiefly of

costly articles of apparel, a specious though irresistible bribery, which had the desired effect. Great numbers of the Moorish doctors came over at once and their example was speedily followed by many of their illiterate disciples. So great was the number of converts that no less than three thousand presented themselves for baptism in one day, and as the rite could not be administered individually, they were christened wholesale by sprinkling them from a mop or hyssop which had been dipped in holy water, and from which the drops fell upon the proselytes as it was twirled over the heads of the multitude. These early successes stimulated the primate's zeal and he next adopted more violent measures by proceeding to imprison and impose penalties upon all Moors who still stood out against conversion. He was resolved not merely to exterminate heresy, but to destroy the basis of belief contained in the most famous Arabic manuscripts, large quantities of which were collected into great piles and burned publicly in the great squares of the city. Many of these were beautifully executed copies of the Koran; others, treasured theological and scientific works, and their indiscriminate destruction is a blot upon the reputation of the cultivated prelate who had created the most learned university in Spain.

More temperate and cautious people besought Ximenes to hold his hand. But he proceeded pertinaciously, declaring that a tamer policy might serve in temporal matters, but not where the interests of the soul were at stake. If the unbeliever could not be drawn he must be driven into the way of salvation, and he continued with unflinching resolution to arrest all recusants, and throw them into the prisons which were filled to overflowing. Discontent grew rapidly and soon broke into open violence. When an *alguazil* in Granada was leading a woman away as a prisoner, the people rose and released her from custody. The insurrection became general in the city and assumed a threatening aspect. Granada was full of warlike Moors and a mob besieged Ximenes in his house until he was rescued by the garrison of the Alhambra.

The king and queen were much annoyed with Ximenes and condemned his zealous precipitancy, but he was clever enough to vindicate his action and bring the sovereigns to believe that it was imperative that the rebellious Moors must be sharply repressed. Now a long conflict began. Forcible conversion became the order of the day; baptism continued to be performed in the gross upon thousands, the alternative being exile, and numbers were actually deported to Barbary in the royal ships. A fierce civil conflict broke out in the Alpujarras beyond Granada, which required a royal army to quell. The object sought was the welfare of the state by producing uniformity of faith.

Ximenes found a strenuous supporter in Diego Deza, the inquisitor-general, who was eager to

emulate the strictness of his predecessor, Torquemada. Deza was a Dominican who had been at one
time professor of theology and confessor to the
queen. He was by nature and predilection exactly
fitted for his new office upon which he entered with
extensive powers. A bull from Pope Alexander VI
dated 1499 invested him with the title of " Conserv-
ator of the Faith " in Spain.

Deza gave a new constitution to the Holy Office
and prescribed that there should be a general " In-
quest " in places not yet visited, and that edicts
should be republished requiring all persons to lay information against suspected heretics. He stirred up
the zeal of all subordinate inquisitors and was well
served by them, especially by one, Lucero, commonly
called *el Tenebroso,* " the gloomy," whose savage
and ruthless proceedings terrorised Cordova where
he presided. He made a general attack upon the
most respectable inhabitants and arrested great
numbers, many of whom were condemned and executed. Informers crowded Lucero's ante-chamber
bringing monstrous tales of heretical conspiracies to
reëstablish Judaism and subvert the Church. His
familiars dragged the accused from their beds to
answer to these charges and the prisons overflowed.
Cordova was up in arms and many would have offered armed resistance to the Inquisition, but the
more circumspect people, the Bishop and Chapter,
some of the nobility and the municipal council appealed to Deza praying him to remove Lucero. The

inquisitor-general however turned furiously upon
the complainants and caused them to be arrested
as abettors of heresy. Philip I, acting for his wife
Juana, the daughter of Ferdinand and Isabella, was
inclined to listen to the complainants, and suspended
both Deza and Lucero from their functions. But
his sudden death stayed the relief he had promised,
and the tormenting officials returned to renew their
oppression.

The Cordovese would not tamely submit and appealed to force. A strong body of men under the
Marques de Priego attacked the " Holy House,"
broke open the prison and liberated many of those
detained, shutting up the officers of the Inquisition
in their place. Lucero took to flight upon a swift
mule and escaped. Though for a time Deza continued to keep his influence, he was shortly forced
to resign and Cordova became tranquil. Deza's
persecution had spared no one. In the eight years
during which he held office, one account, probably
greatly exaggerated, says that 2,592 persons were
burned alive, some nine hundred were burned in effigy, and thirty-five thousand were punished by
penance, fines and confiscations.

The fall of Deza and the hostile attitude of the
people warned the authorities that the affairs of the
Inquisition must be managed more adroitly. New
inquisitors must be appointed and choice fell upon
Ximenes de Cisneros, who had already played a
foremost part in proselytising, but who now was

willing to adopt more moderate measures. The
Pope in giving his approval sent him a cardinal's
hat as a recompense for past services, and as an encouragement to act wisely in the future. He had a
difficult task. Disaffection, strongly pronounced,
prevailed through the kingdom and the Inquisition
was everywhere cordially detested. Ximenes strove
to appease the bitter feeling by instituting a searching inquiry into the conduct of his immediate predecessor, Deza, and promising to hear all complaints
and redress all grievances. He created a " Catholic
Congregation " as a special court to investigate the
actions of Lucero in the proceedings growing out
of the charges against Archbishop Talavera and his
family. This court in due course pronounced a verdict of acquittal and rehabilitation of the Talaveras.
Ruined houses were rebuilt, the memory of the
dead restored to honour and fame, and this act
of grace was published at Valladolid with great
solemnity in the presence of the kings, bishops and
grandees.

Nevertheless Ximenes had no desire to remodel
the Holy Office or limit its operations to any considerable extent. On the contrary, he bent all his
efforts to develop its influence and make it an engine of government, utilising it as a political as well
as a religious agency. It was as rigorous as ever but
he set his face like a flint against dishonesty. He
systematised the division of the realm into inquisi-
torial provinces, each under its own inquisitor with

headquarters in the principal cities, such as Seville, Toledo, Valladolid, Murcia, and in Sardinia and Sicily beyond the seas. His personal ascendancy became extraordinary. He enjoyed the unbounded confidence and favour of the sovereign. He had been created Cardinal of Spain, a title rarely conferred. As archbishop of Toledo, he was the supreme head of the Spanish clergy, and as inquisitor-general, he was the terror of every priest and every layman within his jurisdiction. He had, in fact, reached the highest ecclesiastical rank, short of the papacy and as he rose higher and higher he wielded powers little short of an independent absolute monarch, and his zeal in the cause of his religion grew more and more fervent and far-reaching. No doubt in an earlier age he would have turned crusader, but now he sought to crush the fugitive Moors who had escaped into Northern Africa, whence they made constant descents upon the south of Spain, burning to avenge the wrongs of their co-religionists, and were a constant scourge and source of grievous trouble.

The evils centred in the province of Oran, a fortified stronghold — the most considerable of the Moslem possessions on the shores of the Mediterranean — whence issued a swarm of pirate cruisers, manned by the exiles driven out of Spain, who had sought and found a welcome refuge in Oran. Ximenes was resolved to seize and sweep out this hornets' nest and undertook its conquest on his own account. Much ridicule was levelled at this "monk about to fight the battles of Spain," but he went forth undeterred at the head of a powerful army, conveyed by a strong fleet from Cartagena, which he landed at the African port of Mazalquivir, and after some desperate fighting made himself master of Oran. After his successful African campaign he resumed his duties of chief inquisitor, and the Holy Office under his fierce and vigorous rule became more than ever oppressive. Ximenes pursued his unwavering course and encouraged his inquisitors in their unceasing activity. He desired to extend the power and influence of the Inquisition, and established it in the new countries recently added to the Spanish dominion. A branch was set up in the newly conquered province of Oran, and another farther afield in the recently discovered new world beyond the Atlantic. On the initiative of Ximenes Fray Juan Quevedo, Bishop of Cuba, was appointed chief inquisitor in the kingdom of Terrafirma, as the territories of the new world were styled.

The energetic pursuit of heresy did not monopolise the exertions of Ximenes. He founded the great University of Alcalá, a vast design, a noble seat of learning richly endowed with magnificent buildings and a remarkable scheme of education, which produced the ablest and most eminent scholars. Another great monument is the well known polyglot Bible, designed to exhibit the scriptures in their various ancient languages, a work of singular erudition upon which the munificent cardinal expended vast sums.

Ximenes lived to the advanced age of eighty-one, long enough to act as regent of Spain during the interregnum preceding the arrival of Charles I, better known as the Emperor Charles V. The immediate cause of his death was said to have been the receipt of a letter from the Emperor in which he was coldly thanked for his services and desired to retire to his diocese, to " seek from heaven that reward which heaven alone could adequately bestow." In his last moments he is reported to have said, " that he had never intentionally wronged any man; but had rendered to every one his due, without being swayed, as far as he was conscious, by fear or affection."

He combined a versatility of talent usually found only in softer and more flexible characters. Though bred in the cloister, he distinguished himself both in the cabinet and the camp. For the latter, indeed, so repugnant to his regular profession, he had a natural genius, according to the testimony of his biographer; and he evinced his relish for it by declaring that " the smell of gunpowder was more grateful to him than the sweetest perfume of Arabia!" In every situation, however, he exhibited the stamp of his peculiar calling; and the stern lineaments of the monk were never wholly concealed under the mask of the statesman or the visor of the warrior. He had a full measure of the religious bigotry which belonged to the age; and he had melancholy scope for displaying it, as chief of that dread tribunal over which he presided during the last ten years of his life.

The accession of the grandson of Ferdinand and Isabella to the Spanish throne as Charles I (better known as the Emperor Charles V), seemed to foreshadow a change in the relations of the Inquisition and the state. The young sovereign was born in Ghent and was more Fleming than Spaniard. Though his grandfather left in his will solemn injunctions " to labour with all his strength to destroy and extirpate heresy " and to appoint ministers " who will conduct the Inquisition justly and properly for the service of God and the exaltation of the Catholic faith, and who will also have great zeal for the destruction of the sect of Mahomet," it was reported that he sympathised with the critics of the Inquisition and was disposed to curtail its activity. The influence of his old tutor, Adrian of Utrecht, whom he commissioned inquisitor-general, first of Aragon, and, after the death of Ximenes, of Castile also, changed him however into a strong friend and staunch supporter of the institution.

Cardinal Manrique, who followed as inquisitor-general, was a man of more kindly disposition, charitable and a benefactor to the poor. He was inclined to relax the severities of the Holy Office but it was urged upon him that heresy was on the increase on account of the appearance of Lutheran

opinions and the bitterest persecution was more than
ever essential. Protestants began to appear sporadi-
cally and called for uncompromising repression.
The writings of Luther, Erasmus, Melancthon,
Zwingli, and the rest of the early reformers were
brought into Spain, but the circulation was adjudged
a crime, though Erasmus had once been a favourite
author.

The Inquisition later prepared an *Index Expur-
gandorum,* or list of condemned and prohibited literature. All books named on it were put
under the ban of the law. Possession of a translation of the Bible in the vulgar tongues was forbidden in 1551, and the prohibition was not lifted until
1782. By that time there was no longer such keen
interest in its contents, and the Book was little circulated. In 1825 the British and Foreign Bible
Society sent one of its agents into Spain to dis-
tribute it, and his adventures are described autobi-
ographically in that interesting work, George Borrow's " Bible in Spain."

In spite of all the efforts to make good Catholics
and good Spaniards of the Moriscos, little real progress was made. They had accepted baptism under
compulsion, not realising that thereby they were
brought under control of the Church. Little effort
was made to instruct them, moreover, and as a result thousands, nominally Christians, observed scru-
pulously the whole Moslem ritual, used the old language, and kept their old costume. Some, to be

sure, were hardly to be distinguished from the Spaniards with whom they had intermarried, but, on the whole, they seemed an unassimilable element in the population.

When Philip II succeeded his father, Charles V, in 1556, he determined to take strong measures. A decree proclaimed in Granada in 1566 forbade the use of the distinctive dress and of the Moorish names. The old customs were to be abandoned, and all the baths were to be destroyed. Rebellion followed this edict, and, for a time, it was doubtful whether it could be crushed. Finally open resistance was overcome, and several thousand were transferred to the mountains of Northern Spain. Meanwhile the Inquisition was active, and thousands were brought to trial for pagan practices.

Prejudice continued to grow, and fanatics declared that Spain could never prosper until the " evil seed " was destroyed or expelled from the Christian land. Jealousy of the prosperity of the Moriscos led the populace to agree with the bigots, and finally expulsion was unanimously decreed by the Council of State, in 1609, during the reign of Philip III. Valencia was first purged, and next Murcia, Granada, Andalusia, Old and New Castile and Aragon. Afterward vigorous attempts to root out individuals of Moorish blood, who had become indistinguishable because of their strict conformity, were made. Great suffering was incurred by the unfortunate exiles and many died. Those who reached Africa carried with them a hatred which persists to the present.

The number driven out is uncertain. The estimates vary from three hundred thousand to three million. Probably the most accurate estimate is that of six hundred thousand. In this number were included the most skilful artisans, and the most industrious and most thrifty portion of the population. It was a mistake from which Spain has never recovered.

CHAPTER III

PRISONS AND PUNISHMENTS

Prisons, usually, a part of the building occupied by court —
Better than civil prisons — Torture inflicted — No new
methods invented — Description of various kinds — Two
Lutheran congregations broken up — Description of some
famous *autos da fé* — Famous victims — Englishmen punished — Archbishop Carranza's trial.

THE prisons of the Inquisition fall under two
great heads, the " secret prisons " in which those
awaiting trial were confined, and the " penitential
prisons " where sentences were served. Generally
there were also *cárceles de familiares* where officers
of the institution charged with wrong-doing were
confined. In some tribunals there were others vari-
ously called *cárceles medias, cárceles comunes,* and
cárceles públicas, where offenders not charged with
heresy might be confined.

The secret prisons, however, have most fired the
imagination. A man might disappear from his accustomed haunts, and for years his family and
friends be ignorant of his condition, or even of his
very existence, until one day he might appear at an
auto da fé. What went on within the walls was a

mystery. Seldom did any hint of the proceedings leak out. Everyone was sworn to secrecy, and the arm of the Inquisition was long, if the luckless witness or attendant failed to heed his instructions.

These prisons were almost invariably a part of the building occupied by the tribunal. In Valencia, it was the archbishop's palace; in Saragossa, the royal castle; in Seville, the Triana; in Cordova, the Alcázar, and so on. In some, there were cells and dungeons already prepared, in others, they were constructed. There was no common standard of convenience or sanitation. In many cases, generally, perhaps, they were superior to the common jails in which ordinary prisoners were confined. Yet we know that some were entirely dark and very damp. Others were so small that a cramped position was necessary, and were hardly ventilated at all. Sometimes they were poorly cared for, and loathsome filth and vermin made them unendurable. Many places were used for prisons during the three hundred years of the Inquisition, and no statement is broad enough to cover them all. The mortality was high, yet not so high as in the prisons generally. Since many were unsuitable and often unsafe, the wearing of fetters was common. Prisoners often, incidentally, speak of their chains.

Occasionally more than one prisoner occupied the same room, and much evidence was secured in this way, as each hoped to lighten his own punishment by inculpating others. Writing materials were permitted, though every sheet of paper must be accounted for and delivered into an official's hands. Lights were not permitted however.

Yet entire secrecy was not always secured. Attendants were sometimes bribed, and by various ingenious methods, communications occasionally found their way in or out. Again in cases of severe sickness, the prisoner might be transferred to a hospital, which however must account for him if he recovered. Cardinal Adrian, the inquisitor-general, reminded the tribunals that the prison was for detention, not for punishment, that prisoners must not be defrauded of their food, and that the cells must be carefully inspected.

These and similar instructions issued at intervals were not always obeyed, for inquisitors were often negligent. According to Lea, " no general judgment can be formed as to the condition of so many prisons during three centuries, except that their average standard was considerably higher than that in other jurisdictions, and that, if there were abodes of horror, such as have been described by imaginative writers they were wholly exceptional." [1] Again the same author quotes instances where prisoners speak of improved health, due to better food in prison than they were accustomed to at home, and in summing up declares that the general management was more humane than could be found elsewhere, either in or out of Spain.

[1] Lea. History of the Inquisition in Spain. Vol. II. p. 526.

We may briefly recapitulate the various processes
of the Inquisition in order, as they obtained. First
came the denunciation, followed by seizure and the
commencement of an inquiry. The several offences
imputed were next submitted to those logical experts
named " qualifiers " who decided, so to speak,
" whether there was a true bill," in which case the
procurator fiscal committed the accused to durance.
Three audiences were given him, and the time was
fully taken up with cautions and monitions. The
charges were next formulated but with much pro-
lixity and reduplication. They were not reduced to
writing and delivered to the accused for slow pe-
rusal and reply, but were only read over to him,
hurriedly. On arraignment he was called upon to
reply, then and there, to each article, to state at once
whether it was true or false. The charges were
usually originated by an informer and resort was
had, if necessary, to " inquiry," the hunting up of
suspicious or damaging facts on which evidence was
sought, in any quarter and from any one good or
bad. If the accused persisted in denial he was allowed counsel, but later the counsel became an official of the Inquisition and naturally made only a
perfunctory defence. An appeal to torture was had
if the prisoner persisted in denying his guilt, in the
face of plausible testimony, or if he confessed only
partially to the charges against him, or if he refused
to name his accomplices. A witness who had re-
tracted his testimony or had contradicted himself,

might be tortured in order that the truth might be made known.

It was admitted, however, that torture was by no means an infallible method for bringing out the truth. "Weak-hearted men, impatient of the first pain, will confess crimes they never committed and criminate others at the same time. Bold and strong ones will bear the most severe torments. Those who have been already on the rack are likely to bear it with greater courage, for they know how to adapt their limbs to it and can resist more powerfully." It may be admitted that the system was so far humane that the torture was not applied until every other effort had been tried and had failed. The instruments of torture were first exhibited with threats, but when once in use, it might be repeated day after day, "in continuation," as it was called, and if any "irregularity" occurred, such as the death of a victim, the inquisitors were empowered to absolve one another. Nobles were supposedly exempted from torture, and it was not permissible by the civil laws in Aragon, but the Holy Office was nevertheless authorised to torture without restriction all persons of all classes.

Torture was not inflicted as a punishment by the Inquisition, nor was it peculiar to its trials. Until a comparatively recent date it was a recognised method of securing testimony, accepted in nearly all courts of Europe as a matter of course. The Inquisition seems to have invented no new methods, and seldom used the extreme forms commonly practised. In fact in nearly every case, torture was inflicted by the regular public executioner who was called in for the purpose and sworn to secrecy. The list of tortures practised on civil prisoners was long, and they seem to us now fiendish in their ingenuity. A complete course would require many hours, and included apparently the infliction of pain to every organ or limb and to almost every separate muscle and nerve. The records of the Inquisition show almost invariably the infliction of a few well known sorts.

Some sorts were abandoned because of the danger of permanent harm, and others less violent, but probably no less painful, were substituted. Often the record states that the prisoner " overcame the torture," *i. e.* was not moved to confess. Evidently, though the whole idea is abhorrent to us to-day, torture as inflicted was less awful than some writers would have us believe.[1]

A curious memento of the methods employed by the Holy Office has been preserved in an ancient " Manual of the Inquisition of Seville," a thin quarto volume bound in vellum, with pages partly printed, partly in manuscript. It bears the date 1628, and purports to be compiled from ancient and modern instructions for the order of procedure. It was found in the Palace of the Inquisition at Seville, when it was sacked in the year 1820. One part of this manual details the steps to be taken, " when

[1] Lea. History of the Inquisition in Spain. Vol. III.

torture has to be performed." The criminal having been brought into the audience, was warned that he had not told the entire truth, and as he was believed to have kept back and hidden many things, he was about to be " tormented " to compel him to speak out. Formal sentence to the torture chamber was then passed, after " invoking the name of Christ." It was announced that the " question " would be administered. The method of infliction was detailed whether by pulleys or by water or cords, or by all, to be continued for " as long a time as may appear well," with the proviso that if in the said torment, " he (or she) should die or be wounded, or if there be any effusion of blood or mutilation of member, the blame should be his (or hers) not ours."

Here follows in manuscript the description of the torments applied to one unfortunate female whose name is not given.

" On this she was ordered to be taken to the chamber of Torment whither went the Lords Inquisitors, and when they were there she was admonished to tell the truth and not to let herself be brought into such great trouble.

" Her answer is not recorded.

" Carlos Felipe, the executor of Justice, was called and his oath taken that he would do his business well and faithfully and that he would keep the secret. All of which he promised.

" She was told to tell the truth or orders would

be given to strip her. She was commanded to be stripped naked.

" She was told to tell the truth or orders would be given to cut off her hair. It was taken off and she was examined by the doctor and surgeon who certified that there was no reason why she should not be put to the torture.

" She was commanded to mount the rack and to tell the truth or her body should be bound; and she was bound. She was commanded to tell the truth, or they would order her right foot to be made fast to the *trampazo*." [1]

After the *trampazo* of the right foot that of the left followed. Then came the binding and stretching of the right arm, then that of the left. After that the *garrote* or the compression of the fleshy parts of the arms and thighs with fine cords, a plan used to revive any person who had fainted under the torture. Last of all the *mancuerda* was inflicted, a simultaneous tension of all the cords on all the limbs and parts.

The water torture was used to extort confession. The patient was tightly bound to the *potro*, or ladder, the rungs of which were sharp-edged. The head was immovably fastened lower than the body, and the mouth was held open by an iron prong. A strip of linen slowly conducted water into the mouth,

---

[1] *Trampazo* means, exactly, an "extreme tightening of cords": *La ultima de las vueltas que se dan en el tormento de las cuerdas.*

causing the victim to strangle and choke. Sometimes six or eight jars, each holding about a quart,
were necessary to bring the desired result. This
is the "water-cure" found in the Philippines by
American soldiers when the islands were captured.

If these persuasions still failed of effect, or if the
hour was late, or "for other considerations" the
torment might be suspended with the explanation
that it had been insufficiently tried and the victim
was taken back to his prison to be brought out again
after a respite. If, on the other hand, a confession
was secured, it was written down word for word
and submitted to the victim for ratification after at
least twenty-four hours had elapsed. If he revoked
the confession, he might be tortured again.

When a number of cases had been decided, the
Suprema appointed a day, usually a Sunday or a
feast day, for pronouncing sentence. This was an
auto da fé, literally an "act of faith." The greater
festivals, Easter day, Christmas day, or Sundays in
Advent or Lent were excepted because these holy
days had their own special musical or dramatic en-
tertainments in the churches. The day fixed was announced from all the pulpits in the city (Seville or
Madrid or Cordova as the case might be) and notice
given that a representative of the Inquisition would
deliver a "sermon of the faith" and that no other
preacher might raise his voice. The civil authorities
were warned to be ready to receive their victims.
At the same time officials unfurled a banner and

made public proclamation to the effect that "no person whatever his station or quality from that hour until the completion of the *auto* should carry arms offensive or defensive, under pain of the greater excommunication and the forfeiture of such arms; nor during the same period should any one ride in coach, or sedan chair, or on horseback, through the streets in the route of the procession, nor enter the enclosure in which the place of execution (*quemadero*) was erected," which was usually beyond the walls.

On the eve of the great day a gorgeous procession was organised, for which all the communities of friars in the city and neighbourhood assembled at the Holy House of the Inquisition, together with the commissaries and familiars of the Holy Office. They sallied forth in triumphal array, followed by the "qualifiers" and experts, all carrying large white tapers, lighted. In their midst a bier was borne covered with a black pall, and, bringing up the rear, was a band, instrumental and vocal, performing hymns. In this order the procession reached the public square, when the pall was removed from the bier and a green cross disclosed which was carried to the altar on the platform, and there erected surrounded by a dozen candles. The white cross was carried to the burning place. Now a strong body of horse and a number of Dominican friars took post to watch through the night and the rest of the actors dispersed. At the same time those who were to suffer were prepared for the fatal event. All were shaved close, both head and beard, so that they might present an appearance of nakedness and humiliation suitable to their forlorn condition. At sunrise on their last day they were arrayed in the prescribed garb and brought from their cells into the chapel or great hall. The least heinous offenders were in coarse black blouses and pantaloons, and were bare-footed and bare-headed. The worst culprits were in the *sanbenito* or penitential sack of yellow canvas, adorned with a St. Andrew's cross in bright red paint, and they often carried a halter round their necks as a badge of ignominy. Those to die at the stake were distinguished by black *sanbenitos* with painted flames and wore on their heads a conical paper headdress in the shape of a bishop's mitre, but also resembling somewhat a fool's cap. This was called the *coroza,* a contemptuous form of *corona* or crown. To make the clothing more hideous, it was decorated by coarse pictures of devils in flames. The condemned as they passed on their way were assailed to the last with importunate exhortations to repent, and a promise was held out to them that if they yielded they would be rewarded by a less painful death, and would be strangled before the flames reached them. All the penitents were obliged to sit upon the ground in profound silence and without so much as moving a limb, while the slow hours dragged themselves along. In the morning a sumptuous meal was set before them, and they were suffered to eat their fill. All the officials and visitors were also regaled before the day's business began.

After the sermon, the secretary read to all the people the oath pledging them to support the Inquisition. Then sentences were pronounced, beginning with the lesser offenders and proceeding to the graver. The punishments ranged from a reprimand, through abjuration, fines, exile, for a longer or shorter period, destruction of residence, penance, scourging, the galleys, imprisonment, wearing the *sanbenito* or penitential garment, up to " relaxation to the secular arm; " *i. e.* death by fire. These penalties carried with them civil disability, and tainted the blood of the descendants of the condemned as well.

Penance might be inflicted in various forms. The condemned, perhaps, might be required to fast one day in every week, to recite a specified number of prayers on appointed days, or to appear at the church door with a halter around his neck on successive Sundays. When scourging was inflicted, the penitent, naked to the waist, was placed astride an ass, and paraded through the principal streets preceded by the town crier. Meanwhile the executioner, accompanied by a clerk to keep tally, plied the *penca* or leather strap, but was charged most solemnly not to draw blood. Usually two hundred lashes was the limit.

Theoretically a heretic who escaped the stake by confession was sentenced to perpetual imprisonment.

This penalty might be served in a prison, a monastery, or in a private house. As a matter of fact, comparatively few were kept in prisons as the expense of maintenance was a heavy burden, and the sentences were usually changed to deportation to the colonies, or assignment to the galleys, or else the sentence was shortened.

The trial and sentence of the bodies of the dead was common, but it was not peculiar to the Inquisition. As late as 1600, in Scotland, the bodies of the Earl of Gowrie and his brother were brought into court, and sentenced to be hanged, quartered and gibbeted. Logan of Restalrig, in 1609, three years after his death, was tried on the charge of being concerned in the same conspiracy, was found guilty and his property was confiscated.

In recounting the punishments imposed by the Inquisition, we must not forget that it assumed jurisdiction over many crimes which to-day are tried by the civil courts. Bigamy was punished as, by a second marriage, the criminal denied the authority of the Church which makes marriage a sacrament. Certain forms of blasphemy also were brought before it, and perjury as well. Personation of the priesthood, or of officials of the Inquisition, was punished, and later it gained jurisdiction over unnatural crimes. Sorcery and witchcraft, which in other states, including the American colonies, were considered subjects for the secular courts, were within the jurisdiction of the Spanish Inquisition.

Strange as it may appear at first thought, the attitude of the Inquisition toward the witchcraft delusion was one of skepticism almost from the beginning. Individual inquisitors, influenced by the well nigh universal belief, were occasionally active, but the Suprema moderated their zeal. In 1610 an *auto* was held at Logroño, which was the centre of wild excitement. Twenty-nine witches were punished, six of whom were burned, and the bones of five others who had died in prison were also consumed. The eighteen remaining were " reconciled." In 1614, however, the Suprema drew up an elaborate code of instructions to the tribunals. While not denying the existence of witchcraft, these instructions treated it as a delusion and practically made proof impossible. As a result of this policy the victims of the craze in Spain can be counted almost by the score, while in almost every other country of Europe, they are numbered by the thousand. In Great Britain the best estimate fixes the number of victims at thirty thousand, and as late as 1775 the great legal author, Sir William Blackstone, says that to deny " the actual existence of witchcraft and sorcery is at once flatly to contradict the revealed word of God." [1]

Heresy, of course, according to the views not only of Catholics but of Protestants, deserved death as a form of treason. Tolerance is a modern idea. Calvin burned Servetus at Geneva and was ap-

[1] Lea. History of the Inquisition in Spain. Vol. IV.

plauded for it. Protestants in England persecuted
other Protestants as well as Catholics. The impenitent heretic in Spain was burned alive. That one,
who after conviction, expressed his repentance, and
his desire to die in the Church was usually strangled
before the flames touched him. Before going on to
describe some famous *autos de fé* and the subsequent
infliction of the death penalty, a word of explanation is in order.

Protestant doctrines were introduced into Spain
either by foreigners or by natives who travelled or
studied in foreign lands, but made slow headway.
In 1557 a secret organisation, comprising about one
hundred and twenty members, was discovered in
Seville. The next year another little band of about
sixty was found in Valladolid.

The almost simultaneous exposure of these two
heretical organisations, both of which included some
prominent people, created great commotion. Charles
V, then living at San Yuste, whither he had retired
after his abdication, wrote to his daughter Juana,
who was acting as regent in the absence of Philip II,
urging the most stringent measures and advocating
that the heretics be pursued mercilessly. Little
stimulation of the Inquisition was necessary, and the
two little congregations were destroyed.

A part of those condemned at Valladolid were
sentenced at a great *auto da fé* held on Trinity Sunday, May 21st, 1559, in Valladolid, not before
Philip II, who was abroad, but his sister, Princess

Juana, presided and with her was the unhappy
Prince, Don Carlos. It was a brilliant gathering, a
great number of grandees of Spain, titled noblemen
and gentlemen untitled, ladies of high rank in gorgeous apparel, all seated in great state to watch the
arrival of the penitential procession. Fourteen heretics were to die, sixteen more to be " reconciled "
but to be branded with infamy and suffer lesser
punishments. Among the sufferers were many persons of rank and consideration such as the two
brothers Cazalla and their sister, children of the
king's comptroller, one of them a canon of the
Church, the other a presbyter, and all three members
of the little Lutheran congregation. Their mother
had died in heresy and on this occasion her effigy,
clad in her widow's weeds and wearing a mitre with
flames, was paraded through the streets and then
burned publicly. Her house, where Lutherans had
met for prayer, was razed to the ground and a pillar
erected with an inscription setting forth her offence
and sentence. Another victim was the licentiate,
Antonio Herrezuelo, an impenitent Lutheran, the
only one who went to the stake unmoved, singing
psalms by the way, and reciting passages of scrip-
ture. They gagged him at last and a soldier in his
zeal stabbed him with his halberd, but the wound
was not mortal and. bleeding and burning, he
slowly expired.

The sixteen who survived the horrors of the day
were haled back to the prison of the Inquisition to

spend one more night in the cells. Next morning
they were again taken before the inquisitors who
exhorted them afresh, and their sentences were
finally read to them. Some destined to the galleys
were transferred first to the civil prison to await removal, after they had been flogged through the
streets and market places. Others clad in the *sanbenito* and carrying ropes were exposed to the hoots
and indignities of the ribald crowd. All who passed
through the hands of the Holy Office were sworn
to seal up in everlasting silence whatever they had
seen, heard or suffered, on peril of a renewed prose-
cution.

Philip II was present at the second great *auto* in
Valladolid in October of the same year, when the
remainder of the Protestants were sentenced. His
wife, Queen Mary of England, was dead, and he
returned to Spain by way of the Netherlands, em-
barking at Flushing for Laredo. Rough weather
and bad seamanship all but wrecked his fleet in sight
of port, and Philip vowed if he were permitted to set
foot on shore, to prosecute the heretics of Spain
unceasingly. He was saved from drowning and
went at once to Valladolid to carry out his
vow.

The ceremony was organised with unprecedented
pomp and splendour. The king came in state,
rejoicing that several notable heretics had been
reserved to die in torments, for his especial delecta-
tion. His heir, Don Carlos, Prince of Asturias, was

also present but under compulsion; he was, at that
time, no more than fourteen years of age and had
writhed with agony at the sight of the suffering at
the former *auto*. Moreover, when called upon to
swear fidelity to the Inquisition, he had taken the
oath with great reluctance. Not so King Philip,
who when called upon to take the same oath at the
second *auto da fé*, rose in his place, drew his sword
and brandished it as he swore to show every favour
to the Holy Office and support its ministers against
whomsoever might directly or indirectly impede its
efforts or affairs. "*Asi lo juro*," he said with deep
feeling. "Thus I swear."

The victims at this great *auto da fé* were many
and illustrious. One was Don Carlos de Seso, an
Italian of noble family, the son of a bishop, a
scholar who had long been in the service of the
Emperor Charles V, and was chief magistrate of
Toro. He had married a Spanish lady and resided
at Logroño, where he became an object of suspicion
as a professor of Lutheranism, and was arrested.
They took him to the prison of Valladolid, where
he was charged, tortured and condemned to die.
When called upon to make confession, he wrote two
full sheets denouncing the Catholic teaching, claim-
ing that it was at variance with the true faith of
the gospel. The priests argued with him in vain,
and he was brought into church next morning,
gagged, and so taken to the burning place, "lest
he should speak heresy in the hearing of the peo-

ple." At the stake the gag was removed and he was again exhorted to recant but he stoutly refused and bade them light up the fire speedily so that he might die in his belief.

Much grief was felt by the Dominicans at the lapse of one of their order, Fray Domingo de Rojas, who was undoubtedly a Lutheran. On his way to the stake he strove to appeal to the king who drove him away and ordered him to be gagged. More than a hundred monks of his order followed him close entreating him to recant, but he persisted in a determined although inarticulate refusal until in sight of the flames. He then recanted and was strangled before being burned. One Juan Sanchez, a native of Valladolid, had fled to Flanders, but was pursued, captured and brought back to Spain to die on this day. When the cords which had bound him snapped in the fire, he bounded into the air with his agony but still repelled the priests and called for more fire. Nine more were burned in the presence of the king, who was no merely passive spectator, but visited the various stakes and ordered his personal guard to assist in piling up the fuel.

The congregation at Seville were sentenced at *autos* held in 1559 and 1560. On December 22d of the latter year, there were fourteen burned in the flesh and three in effigy. The last were notable people. One was Doctor Egidio, who had been a leading canon of Seville Cathedral, and who had been tried and forced to recant his heresies in 1552.

After release he renewed his connection with the Lutherans, but soon died and was buried at Seville. His corpse was exhumed, brought to trial, and burnt with his effigy; all his property was confiscated and his memory declared infamous. Another was Doctor Ponce de la Fuente, a man of deep learning and extraordinary eloquence who had been chaplain and preacher to the emperor. He followed the Imperial Court into Germany, then returned to charm vast congregations in Seville, but his sermons were reported by spies to be tainted with the Reformed doctrines. He was seized by the Inquisition and many incriminating papers were also taken. When cast into a secret dungeon and confronted with these proofs of his heresy, he would make no confession, nor would he betray any of his friends. He was transferred to a subterranean cell, damp and pestiferous, so narrow he could barely move himself, and was deprived of the commonest necessaries of life. Existence became impossible under such conditions, and he died, proclaiming with his last breath that neither Scythians nor cannibals could be more cruel and inhuman than the barbarians of the Holy Office. The third effigy consumed was that of Doctor Juan Pérez de Pineda, then a fugitive in Geneva.

Chief among the living victims was Julian Hernandez, commonly called *el Chico*, " the little," from his diminutive stature. Yet his heart was of the largest and his courage extraordinary. He was a deacon in the Reformed Church and dared to penetrate the interior of Spain, disguised as a muleteer, carrying merchandise in which Lutheran literature was concealed. Being exceedingly shrewd and daring he travelled far and wide, beyond Castile into Andalusia, distributing his books among persons of rank and education in all the chief cities. His learning, skill in argument, and piety, were not less remarkable than the diligence and activity by which he baffled all efforts to lay hold of him. At last he was caught and imprisoned. Relays of priests were told off to controvert his opinions, and he was repeatedly tortured to extract the names of those who had aided him in his long and dangerous pilgrimage through the Peninsula, but he was staunch and silent to the last.

A citizen of London, one Nicholas Burton, was a shipmaster who traded to Cadiz in his own vessel. He was arrested on the information of a " familiar " of the Inquisition, charged with having spoken in slighting terms of the religion of the country. No reason was given him, and when he protested indignantly, he was thrown into the common gaol and detained there for a fortnight, during which he was moved to administer comfort and preach the gospel to his fellow-prisoners. This gave a handle to his persecutors and he was removed on a further charge of heresy to Seville, where he was imprisoned, heavily ironed in the secret gaol of the Inquisition in the Triana. At the end he was condemned as a

contumacious Lutheran, and was brought out, clad
in the *sanbenito* and exposed in the great hall of
the Holy Office with his tongue forced out of his
mouth. Last of all, being obdurate in his heresy,
he was burned and his ship with its cargo was taken
possession of by his persecutors.

The story does not end here. Another Englishman, John Frampton, an attorney of Bristol, was
sent to Cadiz by a part-owner to demand restoration
of the ship. He became involved in a tedious law
suit and was at last obliged to return to England
for enlarged powers. Bye and bye he went out a
second time to Spain, and on landing at Cadiz was
seized by the servants of the Inquisition and carried
to Seville. He travelled on mule back "tied by a
chain that came three times under its belly and the
end whereof was fastened in an iron padlock made
fast to the saddle bow." Two armed familiars rode
beside him, and thus escorted and secured, he was
conveyed to the old prison and lodged in a noisome
dungeon. The usual interrogatories were put to
him and it was proved to the satisfaction of the Holy
Office that he was an English heretic. The same
evidence sufficed to place him on the rack, and after
fourteen months, he was taken to be present as a
penitent at the same *auto da fé* which saw Burton,
the ship's captain, done to death. Frampton went
back to prison for another year and was forbidden
to leave Spain. He managed to escape and returned
to England to make full revelation of his wrongs,

but the ship was never surrendered and no indemnity was obtained.

Other Englishmen fell from time to time into the hands of the Inquisition. Hakluyt preserved the simple narratives of two English sailors, who were brought by their Spanish captors from the Indies as a sacrifice to the "Holy House" of Seville, though the authenticity of the statement has been attacked. One, a happy-go-lucky fellow, Miles Phillips, who had been too well acquainted in Mexico with the dungeons of the Inquisition, slipped over the ship's side at San Lucar, near Cadiz, made his way to shore, and boldly went to Seville, where he lived a hidden life as a silk-weaver, until he found his chance to steal away and board a Devon merchantman. The other, Job Hortop, added to his two years of Mexican imprisonment, two more years in Seville. Then "they brought us out in procession," as he tells us, "every one of us having a candle in his hand and the coat with S. Andrew's cross on our backs; they brought us up on an high scaffold, that was set up in the place of S. Francis, which is in the chief street in Seville; there they set us down upon benches, every one in his degree and against us on another scaffold sate all the Judges and the Clergy on their benches. The people wondered and gazed on us, some pitying our case, others said, 'Burn those heretics.' When we had sat there two hours, we had a sermon made to us, after which one called Bresina, secretary to the In-

quisition, went up into the pulpit with the process
and called on Robert Barret, shipmaster, and John
Gilbert, whom two familiars of the Inquisition
brought from the scaffold in front of the Judges,
and the secretary read the sentence, which was that
they should be burnt, and so they returned to the
scaffold and were burnt.

"Then, I, Job Hortop and John Bone, were
called and brought to the same place, as the others
and likewise heard our sentence, which was, that
we should go to the galleys there to row at the
oar's end ten years and then to be brought back
to the Inquisition House, to have the coat with St.
Andrew's cross put on our backs and from thence
to go to the everlasting prison remediless.

"I, with the rest were sent to the Galleys, where
we were chained four and four together. . . .
Hunger, thirst, cold and stripes we lacked none, till
our several times expired; and after the time of
twelve years, for I served two years above my sentence, I was sent back to the Inquisition House in
Seville and there having put on the above mentioned
coat with St. Andrew's cross, I was sent to the everlasting prison remediless, where I wore the coat
four years and then, upon great suit, I had it taken
off for fifty duckets, which Hernandez de Soria,
treasurer of the king's mint, lent me, whom I was
to serve for it as a drudge seven years." This victim, too, escaped in a fly-boat at last and reached
England.

The records of the Inquisition of this period contain the name of an eminent Spanish ecclesiastic who offended the Holy Office and felt the weight of its arm.   This was Bartolome de Carranza, Archbishop of Toledo, Primate of Spain, a Dominican, — whose rise had been rapid and who was charged with leanings toward Lutheranism.   In early life he had passed through the hands of the Inquisition and was censured for expressing approval of the writings of Erasmus, but no other action was taken. His profound theological knowledge indeed commended him to the Councils of the Church, for which he often acted as examiner of suspected books.

Carranza's connection with English history is interesting.   At the time of Queen Mary's marriage with Philip II, he came to London to arrange, in conjunction with Cardinal Pole, for the reconciliation of England to Rome.   He laboured incessantly to win over British Protestants, " preached continually, convinced and converted heretics without number, . . . guided the Queen and Councils and assisted in framing rules for the governance of the English Universities."   He was particularly anxious for the persecution of obstinate heretics, and was in a measure responsible for the burning of Thomas Cranmer, Archbishop of Canterbury.   His zeal and his great merits marked him down as the natural successor to the archbishopric of Toledo, when it became vacant, and he was esteemed as a

chief pillar of the Catholic Church, destined in due
course to the very highest preferment. He might
indeed become cardinal and even supreme pontiff
before he died.

Yet when nearing the topmost pinnacle he was on
the verge of falling to the lowest depths. He had
many enemies. His stern views on Church discipline, enunciated before the Council of Trent, alien-
ated many of the bishops, who planned his ruin and
secretly watched his discourses and writings for
symptoms of unsoundness. Valdés, the chief inquisitor, was a leading opponent and industriously
collected a mass of evidence tending to inculpate
Carranza. He had used " perilous language " when
preaching in England, especially in the hearing of
heretics, and one witness deposed that some of his
sermons might have been delivered by Melancthon
himself. He had affirmed that mercy might be
shown to Lutherans who abjured their errors, and
had frequently manifested scandalous indulgence to
heretics. Valdés easily framed a case against Carranza, strong enough to back up an application to
the pope to authorise the Inquisition to arrest and
imprison the primate of Spain. Paul IV, the new
pope, permitted the arrest. Great circumspection
was shown in making it because of the prisoner's
rank. Carranza was invited to come to Valladolid
to have an interview with the king, and, with some
misgivings, the archbishop set out. A considerable
force of men was gathered together by the way —

all loyal to the Inquisition — and at the town of
Torrelaguna, the arrest was made with great formality and respect.

On reaching Valladolid the prisoner begged he
might be lodged in the house of a friend. The Holy
Office consented but hired the building. The trial
presented many serious difficulties. Here was no
ordinary prisoner; Carranza was widely popular,
and the Supreme Council of the Kingdom was divided as to the evidences of his guilt. Nearly a
hundred witnesses were examined, but proof was
not easily to be secured. Besides, Carranza had appealed to the Supreme Pontiff. Year after year was
spent in tiresome litigation and a fierce contest ensued between Rome and the Spanish court which
backed up the Inquisition. At length, after eight
years' confinement, the primate was sent to Cartagena to take ship for Rome, accompanied by several
inquisitors and the Duke of Alva, that most notorious nobleman, the scourge and oppressor of the
Netherlands. All landed at Civita Vecchia and the
party proceeded to the Holy City, when Carranza
was at once lodged in the Castle of St. Angelo, the
well known State prison. He was detained there
nine years, until released by Pope Gregory XIII. He
was censured for his errors, and required to abjure
the Lutheran principles found in his writings, and
was relieved from his functions as archbishop, to
which, however, his strength, impaired by age and
suffering, was no longer equal. While visiting the

seven churches as a penance, he was taken ill, April 23d, 1576, and soon died. Before his death, however, the pope gave him full indulgence.

Those who saw him in his last days record that he bore his trials with dignity and patience. But this learned priest who had been called to the highest rank of the ecclesiastical hierarchy, only to be himself assailed and thrown down, was the same who had sat in cruel judgment upon Thomas Cranmer and compassed his martrydom.

CHAPTER IV

THE INQUISITION ABROAD

THE acquisition of Spanish America opened a fresh field for the activity of the Inquisition. Besides the natives there were the New Christians who had fled across the seas seeking refuge from intolerance in the old country. Although the emigration of heretics was forbidden after a time, lest they should spread the hateful doctrines, Cardinal Ximenes, when inquisitor-general, resolved that the New World should have its own Holy Office, and appointed Fray Juan de Quevedo, then Bishop of Cuba, as inquisitor-general of the " Tierra Firma " as the Spanish mainland was commonly called. The Inquisition was more broadly established by Charles V, who empowered Cardinal Adrian to organise it and appoint new chiefs. The Dominicans were supreme, as in the old country, and proceeded with their usual fiery vigour, wandering at large through the new territories and spreading dismay among the native population. The Indians retreated in crowds into the interior, abandoned the Christianity they had never really embraced, and joined the other native tribes still unsubdued. The Spanish viceroys alarmed at the general desertion complained to the king at home and the excessive zeal of the inquisitors was checked for a time. But when Philip II came into power he would not agree with this milder policy, and although the inquisitors were no longer permitted to perambulate the country districts hunting up heretics, the Holy Office was established with its palaces and prisons in the principal cities and acted with great vigour. Three great central tribunals were created at Panama, Lima, and at Cartagena de las Indias, and persecution raged unceasingly, chiefly directed against Jews and Moors. In the city of Mexico also there was an inquisitor-general. A royal edict proclaimed that "no one newly converted to our Holy Faith from being Moor or Jew nor his child shall pass over into our Indies without our express license." At the same time the prohibition was extended to any who had been "reconciled," and to the child or grandchild of anyone who had worn the *sanbenito* or of any person burnt or condemned as a heretic . . . "all, under penalty of loss of goods and peril of his person, shall be perpetually banished from the Indies, and if he have no property let them give him a hundred lashes, publicly."

The emperor, Charles V, is responsible for the extension of the Inquisition from Spain to the Low Countries, by which he repaid the loyal service and devotion the Dutch people had long rendered him. This Inquisition was headed at first however by a layman, and then four inquisitors chosen from the secular clergy were named. The Netherlanders resisted stoutly its establishment and its operation, and in 1646 it was provided that no sentence should go into effect unless approved by some member of the provincial council. Heretics were condemned of course, but the number was not large, though in some way grossly exaggerated reports of the numbers of victims have gained credence. Finally, on the application of the people of Brabant, who declared that the name would injure commercial prosperity in their district, the name was dropped altogether. At best it was a faint and feeble copy of the Spanish institution, and during the reign of Charles was little feared. In proof we may cite the fact that eleven successive edicts were necessary to keep the Inquisition at work between 1620 and 1650.

Philip II, on his accession, attempted to increase the power of the institution, with the hope of uprooting the reformed doctrines. The assertion, often made, however, that the Inquisition is responsible for the revolt of the Netherlands is entirely too broad. Other factors than religious differences

entered into the complex situation. The terrible war
which finally resulted in the independence of the
Protestant Netherlands, falls outside the plan of this
volume.

Philip wished to extend the sway of the Inquisition and planned a naval tribunal to take cognisance
of heresy afloat. He created the Inquisition of the
Galleys, or, as it was afterwards styled, of the Army
and Navy. In every sea port a commissary general
visited the shipping to search for prohibited books
and make sure of the orthodoxy of crews and passengers. Even cargoes and bales of merchandise
were examined, lest the taint of heresy should infect
them. This marine inspection was most active in
Cadiz, at that time the great centre of traffic with the
far West. A visitor from the Holy Office with a
staff of assistants and familiars boarded every ship
on arrival and departure and claimed that their authority should be respected, so that nothing might
be landed or embarked without their certificate.
The merchants resented this system which brought
substantial commercial disadvantages, and the ships'
captains disliked priestly interference with their
crews, whose regular duties were neglected. The
men were kept below under examination, when they
were wanted on deck to make or shorten sail or take
advantage of a change in the wind or a turn in the
tide. By degrees the marine Inquisition was
thought to impede business on the High Seas and
fell into disuse.

Under succeeding sovereigns the Holy Office was still favoured and supported, but the reign of Philip III witnessed loud and frequent remonstrances against its operation. The Cortes of Castile implored the king to put some restraint upon the too zealous inquisitors, but they still wielded their arbitrary powers unchecked, and Philip sought further encouragement for them from Rome. The accession of Philip IV to the throne was celebrated by an *auto da fé,* but no victim was put to death, and the only corporal punishment inflicted was the flogging of an immoral nun who professed to have made a compact with the devil. She was led out gagged, and, wearing the *sanbenito,* received two hundred lashes followed by perpetual imprisonment. Philip IV strove for a time to check the activity of the Inquisition, but he was too weak and wavering to make permanent headway against an institution, the leaders of which knew precisely what they were striving for, and pertinaciously pursued it.

A graphic account of what purport to have been the painful experiences of a poor soul who fell at a later date into the clutches of the inquisitors is related by himself in a curious pamphlet printed in Seville, by one Carcel, who was a goldsmith in that city. Evidently there is the work of another hand in it, however, as it is written with too much regard for the dramatic to have been his own composition. The description of the *auto* is also unusual, and not according to the usual procedure.

He says that he was arrested on the 2nd of April, 1680, at ten o'clock in the evening, as he was finishing a gold necklace for one of the queen's maids of honour. A week after his first arrest Carcel was examined. We will quote his own words: —

"In an ante-room," he says, "a smith frees me of my irons and I pass from the ante-chamber to the 'Inquisitor's table,' as the small inner room is called. It is hung with blue and citron-coloured taffety. At one end, between the two grated windows, is a gigantic crucifix and on the central estrade (a table fifteen feet long surrounded by armchairs), with his back to the crucifix, sits the secretary, and on my right, Francisco Delgado Ganados, the Grand Inquisitor, who is a secular priest. The other inquisitors had just left, but the ink was still wet in their quills, and I saw on papers before their chairs some names marked with red ink. I am seated on a low stool opposite the secretary. The inquisitor asks my name and profession and why I come there, exhorting me to confess as the only means of quickly regaining my liberty. He hears me, but when I fling myself weeping at his knees, he says coolly there is no hurry about my case; that he has more pressing business than mine waiting, (the secretary smiles), and he rings a little silver bell which stands beside him on the black cloth, for the alcaide who leads me off down a long gallery, where my chest is brought in and an inventory taken by the secretary. They cut my hair off and

strip me of everything, even to my ring and gold
buttons; but they leave me my beads, my handkerchief and some money I had fortunately sewn in
my garters. I am then led bareheaded into a cell,
and left to think and despair till evening when they
bring me supper.

" The prisoners are seldom put together. Silence
perpetual and strict is maintained in all the cells.
If any prisoner should moan, complain or even pray
too loud, the gaolers who watch the corridors night
and day warn them through the grating. If the
offence is repeated, they storm in and load you with
blows to intimidate the other prisoners, who, in the
deep grave-like silence, hear your every cry and
every blow.

" Once every two months the inquisitor, accompanied by his secretary and interpreter, visits the
prisoners and asks them if their food is brought
them at regular hours, or if they have any complaint to make against the gaolers. But this is only
a parade of justice, for if a prisoner dares to utter
a complaint, it is treated as mere fanciful ravings
and never attended to.

" After two months' imprisonment," goes on Carcel, " one Saturday, when, after my meagre prison
dinner, I give my linen, as usual, to the gaolers to
send to the wash, they will not take it and a great
cold breath whispers at my heart — to-morrow is
the *auto da fé*. When, immediately after the vespers at the cathedral, they ring for matins, which

they never do but when rejoicing on the eve of a
great feast, I know that my horrid suspicions are
right.   Was I glad at my escape from this living
tomb, or was I paralysed by fear, at the pile perhaps
already hewn and stacked for my wretched body?
I know not.   I was torn in pieces by the devils that
rack the brains of unhappy men.   I refused my next
meal, but, contrary to their wont, they pressed it
more than usual.   Was it to give me strength to
bear my torture?   Do God's eyes not reach to the
prisons of the Inquisition?

" I am just falling into a sickly, fitful sleep, worn
out with conjecturing, when, about eleven o'clock at
night, the great bolts of my cell grind and jolt back
and a party of gaolers in black, in a flood of light,
so that they looked like demons on the borders of
heaven, come in.

" The alcaide throws down by my pallet a heap
of clothes, tells me to put them on and hold myself
ready for a second summons.   I have no tongue to
answer, as they light my lamp, leave me and lock
the door behind them.   Such a trembling seizes me
for half an hour, that I cannot rise and look at the
clothes which seem to me shrouds and winding
sheets.   I rise at last, throw myself down before the
black cross I had smeared with charcoal on the wall,
and commit myself, as a miserable sinner, into God's
hands.   I then put on the dress, which consists of
a tunic with long, loose sleeves and hose drawers,
all of black serge, striped with white.

" At two o'clock in the morning the wretches came and led me into a long gallery where nearly two hundred men, brought from their various cells, all dressed in black, stood in a long silent line against the wall of the long, plain vaulted, cold corridor where, over every two dozen heads, swung a high brass lamp. We stood silent as a funeral train. The women, also in black, were in a neighbouring gallery, far out of our sight. By sad glimpses down a neighbouring dormitory I could see more men dressed in black, who, from time to time, paced backwards and forwards. These I afterwards found were men doomed also to be burnt, not for murder — no, but for having a creed unlike that of the Jesuits. Whether I was to be burnt or not I did not know, but I took courage, because my dress was like that of the rest and the monsters could not dare to put two hundred men at once into one fire, though they did hate all who love doll-idols and lying miracles.

" Presently, as we waited sad and silent, gaolers came round and handed us each a long yellow taper and a yellow scapular, or tabard, crossed behind and before with red crosses of Saint Andrew. These are the *sanbenitos* that Jews, Turks, sorcerers, witches, heathen or perverts from the Roman Catholic Church are compelled to wear. Now came the gradation of our ranks — those who have relapsed, or who were obstinate during their accusations, wear the *zamarra*, which is gray, with a man's head

burning on red faggots painted at the bottom and
all round reversed flames and winged and armed
black devils horrible to behold. I, and seventy
others, wear these, and I lose all hope. My blood
turns to ice; I can scarcely keep myself from
swooning. After this distribution they bring us,
with hard, mechanical regularity, pasteboard conical
mitres (*corozas*) painted with flames and devils
with the words '*sorcerer*' and '*heretic*' written round the rim. Our feet are all bare. The
condemned men, pale as death, now begin to weep
and keep their faces covered with their hands, round
which the beads are twisted. God only — by speaking from heaven — could save them. A rough,
hard voice now tells us we may sit on the ground
till our next orders come. The old men and boys
smile as they eagerly sit down, for this small relief
comes to them with the refreshment of a pleasure.

"At four o'clock they bring us bread and figs,
which some drop by their sides and others languidly
eat. I refuse mine, but a guard prays me to put it
in my pocket for I may yet need it. It is as if an
angel had comforted me. At five o'clock, at day-
break, it was a ghastly sight to see shame, fear,
grief, despair, written on our pale livid faces. Yet
not one but felt an undercurrent of joy at the pros-
pect of any release, even by death.

"Suddenly, as we look at each other with ghastly
eyes, the great bell of the Giralda begins to boom
with a funeral knell, long and slow. It was the

signal of the gala day of the Holy Office, it was the
signal for the people to come to the show. We are
filed out one by one. As I pass the gallery in the
great hall, I see the inquisitor, solemn and stern,
in his black robes, throned at the gate. Beneath
him is his secretary, with a list of the citizens of
Seville in his wiry twitching hands. The room is
full of the anxious frightened burghers, who, as
their names are called and a prisoner passes through,
move to his trembling side to serve as his god-
father in the Act of Faith. The honest men shudder
as they take their place in the horrible death procession. The time-serving smile at the inquisitor,
and bustle forward. This is thought an honourable
office and is sought after by hypocrites and suspected
men afraid of the Church's sword.

" The procession commences with the Dominicans. Before them flaunts the banner of the order
in glistening embroidery that burns in the sun and
shines like a mirror, the frocked saint, holding a
threatening sword in one hand, and in the other, an
olive branch with the motto, ' Justitia et miseri-
cordia ' (Justice and mercy). Behind the banner
come the prisoners in their yellow scapulars, holding their lighted torches, their feet bleeding with the
stones and their less frightened godfathers, gay in
cloak and sword and ruff tripping along by their
side, holding their plumed hats in their hands. The
street and windows are crowded with careless eyes,
and children are held up to execrate us as we pass

to our torturing death. The *auto da fé* was always a holiday sight to the craftsmen and apprentices; it drew more than even a bull fight, because of the touch of tragedy about it. Our procession, like a long black snake, winds on, with its banners and crosses, its shaven monks and mitred bare-footed prisoners, through street after street, heralded by soldiers who run before to clear a way for us — to stop mules and clear away fruit-stalls, street-performers and their laughing audiences. We at last reach the Church of All the Saints, where, tired, dusty, bleeding and faint we are to hear mass.

" The church has a grave-vault aspect and is dreadfully like a charnel house. The great altar is veiled in black, and is lit with six silver candlesticks, whose flames shine like yellow stars with clear twinkle and a soft halo round each black, fire-tipped wick. On each side of the altar, that seems to bar out God and his mercy from us and to wrap the very sun in a grave cloak, are two thrones, one for the grand-inquisitor and his counsel, another for the king and his court. The one is filled with sexton-like lawyers, the other with jewelled and feathered men.

" In front of the great altar and near the door where the blessed daylight shines with hope and joy, but not for us, is another altar, on which six gilded and illuminated missals lie open; those books of the Gospels, too, in which I had once read such texts as — God is love; Forgive as ye would be forgiven; Faith, hope, charity: these three, but the greatest of these is charity. Near this lesser altar the monks had raised a balustraded gallery, with bare benches, on which sat the criminals in their yellow and flame-striped tabards with their godfathers. The doomed ones came last, the more innocent first. Those who entered the black-hung church first, passing up nearest to the altar sat there, either praying or in a frightened trance of horrid expectancy. The trembling living corpses wearing the mitres, yellow and red, came last, preceded by a gigantic crucifix, the face turned from them.

"Immediately following these poor mitred men came servitors of the Inquisition, carrying four human effigies fastened to long staves, and four chests containing the bones of those men who had died before the fire could be got ready. The coffers were painted with flames and demons and the effigies wore the dreadful mitre and the crimson and yellow shirt all a-flame with paint. The effigies sometimes represented men tried for heresy since their death and whose estates had since been confiscated and their effigies doomed to be burnt as a warning; for no one within their reach may escape if they differ in opinion with the Inquisition.

"Every prisoner being now in his place — godfathers, torchmen, pikemen, musketeers, inquisitors, and flaunting court — the Provincial of the Augustins mounted the pulpit, followed by his ministrant and preached a stormy, denouncing, exulting sermon, half an hour long (it seemed a month of anguish), in which he compared the Church with burning eloquence to Noah's ark; but with this difference, that those animals who entered it before the deluge came out of it unaltered, but the blessed Inquisition had, by God's blessing, the power of changing those whom its walls once enclosed, turning them out meek as the lambs he saw around him so tranquil and devout, all of whom had once been cruel as wolves and savage and daring as lions.

" This sermon over, two readers mounted the pulpit to shout the list of names of the condemned, their crimes (now, for the first time, known to them) and their sentences. We grew all ears and trembled as each name was read.

" As each name was called the alcaide led out the prisoner from his pen to the middle of the gallery opposite the pulpit, where he remained standing, taper in hand. After the sentence he was led to the altar where he had to put his hand on one of the missals and to remain there on his knees.

" At the end of each sentence, the reader stopped to pronounce in a loud, angry voice, a full confession of faith, which he exhorted us, the guilty, to join with heart and voice. Then we all returned to our places. My offence, I found, was having spoken bitterly of the Inquisition, and having called a crucifix a mere bit of cut ivory. I was therefore declared excommunicated, my goods confiscated to the king, I was banished Spain and condemned to

the Havana galleys for five years with the following
penances: I must renounce all friendship with heretics and suspected persons; I must, for three years,
confess and communicate three times a month; I
must recite five times a day, for three years, the
Pater and Ave Maria in honour of the Five
Wounds; I must hear mass and sermon every Sunday and feast day; and above all, I must guard
carefully the secret of all I had said, heard, or seen
in the Holy Office (which oath, as the reader will
observe, I have carefully kept).

"The inquisitor then quitted his seat, resumed
his robes and followed by twenty priests, each with
a staff in his hand, passed into the middle of the
church and with divers prayers some of us were
relieved from excommunication, each of us receiving a blow from a priest. Once, such an insult
would have sent the blood in a rush to my head, and
I had died but I had given a return buffet; now, so
weak and broken-spirited was I, I burst into tears.

"Now, one by one, those condemned to the stake,
faint and staggering, were brought in to hear their
sentences, which they did with a frightened va-
cancy, inconceivably touching, but the inquisitors
were gossiping among themselves and scarcely
looked at them. Every sentence ended with the
same cold mechanical formula: That the Holy Office being unhappily unable to pardon the prisoners
present, on account of their relapse and impenitence,
found itself obliged to punish them with all the

rigour of earthly law, and therefore delivered them with regret to the hands of secular justice, praying it to use clemency and mercy towards the wretched men, saving their souls by the punishment of their bodies and recommending death, but not effusion of blood. Cruel hypocrites!

" At the word blood the hangmen stepped forward and took possession of the bodies, the alcaide first striking each of them on the chest to show that they were now abandoned to the rope and fire." Then he goes on to describe the scene at the *quemadero,* which, however, included nothing of importance not already mentioned elsewhere.

After the death of Philip IV, and during the minority of his son, Charles II, Father Nithard, a Jesuit, who combined the two forces long in opposition, the disciples of Loyola and the descendants of Torquemada, was for a time inquisitor-general. The Holy Office was hotly opposed by Don John of Austria, a natural son of Philip IV, who rose to political power and would have fallen a victim to the Inquisition had not popular indignation sided with him against Nithard, who fled from Spain to Rome. He was stripped of all his offices but still kept the favour of the queen-mother who finally secured for him from Pope Clement X the coveted cardinal's hat. Don John was unequal to the task of curbing the power of the Inquisition, however, and the institution claimed wider and wider jurisdiction.

Growing dissatisfaction prevailed, and in 1696, the king, Charles II, summoned a conference or Grand Junta to enquire into the complaints that poured in from all quarters against the Inquisition. It was composed of two councillors of state from Castile, Aragon, the Indies, and the Spanish provinces in Italy, with two members of the religious orders. It reported that the Holy Office exercised illegal powers, still arrogated the right to throw persons of rank into prison and cover their families with disgrace. It punished with merciless severity the slightest opposition or disrespect shown to dependents or familiars who had come to enjoy extensive and exorbitant privileges. They claimed secular jurisdiction in matters nowise appertaining to religion, and set aside restrictions contained in their own canon law. The Junta strongly recommended that these restrictions should be rigidly enforced, and that no one should be thrown into the prisons of the Inquisition, save on charges of an heretical nature. It urged the right of appeal to the throne, and the removal of all causes to the royal courts for trial. It detailed the privileges granted to the servants of the Holy Office. Even a coachman or a lackey demanded reverence and might conduct himself with unbounded insolence. If a servant girl were not treated obsequiously in a shop she might complain and the offender was liable to be cast into the dungeons of the Inquisition. So great was the discontent, so many tumults arose, that the Junta

would have all such unrighteous privileges curtailed, and would authorise the civil courts to keep
the encroachments of the Holy Office in check.

With the eighteenth century the authority of the
Holy Office visibly waned. Philip V, a French
prince, and a grandson of Louis XIV, whose succession produced the long protracted war of the
Spanish Succession, declined to be honoured with
an *auto da fé* at his coronation, but he maintained
the Inquisition as an instrument of despotic government, and actually used it to punish as heretics those
who had any doubt concerning his title to the crown.
Yet he rather used the Inquisition than supported
it; for he deprived of his office an inquisitor-general who had presumed to proceed for heresy against
a high officer. The Cortes of Castile again, (1714),
recorded their condemnation, but without any
further benefit than that which must eventually result from the disclosure of a truth. The same body
reiterated their disapproval a few years afterwards,
(1720). But while Philip V used the Inquisition
for his own service, and the heretical doctrine which
had prevailed two centuries before no longer left
a trace behind, there were multitudes of persons
accused of attempting to revive Judaism and others
gave offence by their efforts to promote Free-
masonry. This gave the inquisitors abundant pre-
text for the discharge of their political mission.

During the reigns of Charles III and Charles IV,
a revival of literature and an advance in political

science guided the attention of the clergy and the government to the position of the court of Rome, as well as to the proceedings of the inquisitors. The former of these monarchs nearly yielded to the advice of his councillors to suppress the Inquisition, as well as to expel the Jesuits. He banished the Society, but, in regard to the Inquisition, said: " The Spaniards want it and it gives me no trouble."

Meanwhile death sentences nearly ceased, and once when a good man was sentenced to be delivered to the secular arm, in compliance with the letter of the law, the inquisitors let him go free. By this contrivance Don Miguel Solano, priest of Esco, a town in Aragon, walked out of the prison of the Inquisition in Saragossa, as a maniac, forgiven his heresy, and lived on as a maniac, exempted from priestly ministrations, while every one knew him to be a reasonable man and treated him accordingly. In the end he died, refusing Extreme Unction, and was buried in unconsecrated ground within the walls of the Inquisition on the banks of the Ebro.

CHAPTER V

THE INQUISITION IN PORTUGAL AND INDIA

The Inquisition in Spain abolished by Napoleon's invasion —
Its revival — Persecution of the Freemasons — The "Tri-
bunal of Faith" established — Inquisition in Portugal —The
case of an Englishman who is arrested, tortured and burnt
alive — Difference between the Inquisitions of Spain and
Portugal — The supreme power of the Holy Office in Por-
tugal in the eighteenth century — The terrible earthquake at
Lisbon — Establishment of the Holy Office in India at Goa
— Description of the Inquisition prison at Goa by M. Dellon
— Case of Father Ephrem — His arrest and rescue by the
English from the hands of the inquisitors.

NAPOLEON'S invasion of Spain and the removal
of the young king, Ferdinand VII, to France, put
an end to the Inquisition. When the Emperor took
possession of Madrid, he called upon all public
bodies to submit to his authority, but the Holy
Office refused. Whereupon he issued an order to
arrest the inquisitors, abolish the Inquisition, and
sequestrate its revenues. All Spain did not readily
yield to the French conqueror, and when the Cortes
met in Cadiz they empowered one of the inquisitors,
who had escaped, to reconstitute the tribunal, but it
was never really restored. At the same time, the
governing powers appointed a special commission

to enquire into the legal status of the ancient body, and to decide whether the Inquisition had any legal right to exist. A report was published in 1812, reviewing its whole history and condemning it as incompatible with the liberties of the country. The indictment against it was couched in very vigorous language. It was held to have been guilty of the most harsh and oppressive measures; to have inflicted the most cruel and illegal punishments; " in the darkness of the night it had dragged the husband from the side of his wife, the father from the children, the children from their parents, and none may see the other again until they are absolved or condemned without having had the means of contributing to their defence or knowing whether they had been fairly tried." The result was a law passed by the Cortes to suppress the Inquisition in Spain.

The restoration of Ferdinand VII, at the termination of the war in 1814, gave the Inquisition fresh life. He resented the action taken by the Cortes, arrested its members, and cast them into prison, declaring them to be infidels and rebels, and forthwith issued a decree reviving the tribunal of the Holy Office. Its supreme council met in Seville and persecution was renewed under the new inquisitor-general, Xavier Mier y Campillo, who put out a fresh list of prohibited books, tried to raise revenues and issued a new Edict of Faith. There might have been another *auto da fé* even in the nineteenth century, but informers would not come for-

ward and latter-day victims could not be found.
Dread, nevertheless, prevailed, and numbers fled for
refuge into foreign lands. Fierce energy was directed against the Freemasons, for during the
French occupation, the palace of the Inquisition at
Seville had been used, partly as a common gaol and
partly as a Freemasons' lodge. The members of
the craft who were found in Spain were dealt with
as heretics, and all Freemasons were excommunicated.

For a time the Inquisition languished, although
favoured by the arbitrary régime introduced by
Ferdinand VII, who sought to reinstate it on its
former lines. It was destroyed or at least suspended by the Revolution of 1820, and on his restoration, the king did not reëstablish it, though the
officials still hoped for a better day and continued
to draw their salaries. Some of the bishops established *juntas de fé,* which took up much the same
work, and July 26th, 1826, a poor schoolmaster
Cayetano Ripoll, was hanged for heresy — the last
execution for this crime in Spain. Finally, January
4th, 1834, the Inquisition was definitely abolished,
and the *juntas de fé* were abolished the next year.

The Inquisition extended its influence into the
neighbouring country of Portugal, which was an independent kingdom until conquered by Philip II in
1580. Here persecution prevailed from the fifteenth
century, chiefly of the Jews and new Christians, who
flocked into the country from Spain, and were

treated with great severity.   The Holy Office was
set up in Lisbon under an inquisitor-general, Diego
de Silva, and Portugal was divided into inquisitional districts.   *Autos da fé* were frequent, and on
a scale hardly known in Spain, though the records
are fragmentary.

From among the cases reported, we may quote
that of an Englishman, a native of Bristol, engaged
in commerce in Lisbon, who boldly assaulted the
cardinal archbishop in the act of performing mass.
Gardiner, as fiercely intolerant as those of the domi-
nant religion who were worshipping according to
their own rites, attacked the priest when he elevated
the host, " snatched away the cake with one hand,
trod it under his feet, and with the other overthrew
the chalice."   The congregation, at first utterly
astounded, raised one great cry and fell bodily upon
the sacrilegious wretch, who was promptly stabbed
in the shoulder and haled before the king, who was
present in the cathedral, and forthwith interrogated.
It was thought that he had been instigated by the
English Protestants to this outrageous insult, but
he declared that he had been solely moved by his
abhorrence of the idolatry he had witnessed.   He
was imprisoned and with him all the English in
Lisbon.   So soon as his wound was healed, he was
examined by the Holy Office, tortured and condemned.   Then he was carried to the market place
on an ass and his left hand was cut off; thence he
was taken to the river side and by a rope and pulley

hoisted over a pile of wood which was set on fire. "In spite of the great torment he continued in a constant spirit and the more terribly he burned the more vehemently he prayed." He was in the act of reciting a psalm, when by the use of exceeding violence, the burning rope broke and he was precipitated into the devouring flames.

A fellow lodger of Gardiner was detained in the Inquisition for two years, and was frequently tortured to elicit evidence against other Englishmen, but without avail. A Scotch professor of Greek in the university of Coimbra was charged with Lutheranism, and imprisoned for a year and a half, after which he was committed to a monastery so that he might be instructed by the monks in the true religion. They did not change his views and he was presently set free. Another, an English shipmaster, was less fortunate and was burned alive as a heretic at Lisbon.

It has been observed that, on comparison of the Inquisitions of Spain and Portugal, a certain marked difference was disclosed between them. The same precise rigour of the Spanish inquisitors was not exhibited by the Portuguese. In Portugal the discipline was more savage yet more feeble. Yet in the latter country there was a brutal and more wanton excess in inflicting pain at the *autos da fé*. When convicts were about to suffer they were taken before the Lord Chief Justice to answer the enquiry as to what religion they intended to die in. If the answer was " in the Roman Catholic Apostolic," the order was given that they should be strangled before burning. If in the Protestant, or in any other religion, death in the flames was decreed. At Lisbon the place of execution, as has been said, was at the waterside. A thick stake was erected for each person condemned, with a wide crosspiece at the top against which a crosspiece was nailed to receive the tops of two ladders. In the centre the victim was secured by a chain, with a Jesuit priest on either side, seated on a ladder, who proceeded to exhort him to repentance. If they failed they declared they left him to the devil and the mob roared, " Let the dog's beard be trimmed," in other words, " his face scorched." This was effected by applying an ignited furze bush at the end of a long pole till his face was burned and blackened. The record of the Portuguese Inquisition to 1794 shows a total of one thousand, one hundred and seventy-five relaxed in person, *i. e.* executed, six hundred and thirty-three relaxed in effigy, and twenty-nine thousand, five hundred and ninety penanced.

The Portuguese were the first Europeans to trade with the Far East and, after Vasco de Gama had discovered India, Albuquerque annexed and occupied Goa, which might have become the seat and centre of the great empire which fell at length into British hands.

Portugal sacrificed all power and prosperity to the extirpation of heresy in its new possessions and

was chiefly concerned in the establishment of the
Holy Office in India. The early Portuguese settlers
in the East clamoured loudly for the Inquisition;
the Jesuit fathers who were zealous in their propa-
ganda in India declared that the tribunal was most
necessary in Goa, owing to the prevailing licentiousness and the medley of all nations and superstitions.
It was accordingly established in 1560, and soon
commenced its active operations with terrific vigour.
General baptisms were frequent in this the ecclesiastical metropolis of India, and so were *autos da fé*
conducted with great pomp with many victims.

A light upon the proceedings of the Holy Office
in Goa is afforded by the story told by a French
traveller, M. Dellon, who was arrested at the instance of the Portuguese governor at Damaum, and
imprisoned at Goa in the private prison of the archbishop. " The most filthy," says Dellon, " the darkest and most horrible of any I had ever seen. . . .
It is a kind of cave wherein there is no day seen but
by a very little hole. The most subtle rays of the
sun cannot enter it and there is never any true light
in it. The stench is extreme. . . ." M. Dellon was
dragged before the Board of the Holy Office, seated
in the Holy House, which is described as a great
and magnificent building, " one side of a great space
before the church of St. Catherine." There were
three gates. The prisoners entered by the central
or largest, and ascending a stately flight of steps,
reached the great hall. Behind the principal build-

ing was another very spacious, two stories high and
consisting of a double row of cells. Those on the
ground floor were the smallest, due to the greater
thickness of the walls, and had no apertures for
light or air. The upper cells were vaulted and white-
washed, and each had a small strongly grated window without glass. The cells had double doors, the
outer of which was kept constantly open, an indispensable plan in this climate or the occupant must
have died of suffocation.

The régime was, to some extent, humane. Water
for ablutions was provided and for drinking purposes, food was given sparingly in three daily meals,
but was wholesome in quality. Physicians were at
hand to attend the sick and confessors to wait on
the dying, but they administered no unction, gave
no viaticum, said no mass. If any died, as many
did, his death was unknown to all without. He was
buried within the walls with no sacred ceremony,
and if it was decided that he had died in heresy,
his bones were exhumed to be burnt at the next
act of Faith. While alive he lived apart in all the
strictness of the modern solitary cell. Alone and
silent, for the prisoner was forbidden to speak, he
was not allowed even to groan or sob or sigh aloud.

The Holy Office in Goa was worked on the same
lines as that of Spain as already described and by
the same officers. There was the *Inquisidor Mor*
or grand-inquisitor, a secular priest, a second or
assistant inquisitor, a Dominican monk, with many

deputies; "qualifiers," to examine books and writings; a fiscal and a procurator; notaries and familiars. The authority of the tribunal was absolute in Goa except that the great officials, archbishop and his grand-vicar, the viceroy and the governor, could not be arrested without the sanction of the supreme council in Lisbon. The procedure, the examination and use of torture was exactly as in other places.

M. Dellon was taxed with having spoken ill of the Inquisition, and was called upon to confess his sins, being constantly brought out and again relegated to his cell and continually harassed to make him accuse himself, until in a frenzy of despair he resolved to commit suicide by refusing food. The physician bled him and treated him for fever, but he tore off the bandages hoping to bleed to death. He was taken up insensible, restored by cordials, and carried before the inquisitor, where he lay on the floor and was assailed with bitter reproaches, heavily ironed and sent back to languish in his cell in a wild access of fury approaching madness.

At last the great day of the Act of Faith approached, and Dellon heard on every side the agonised cries of both men and women. During the night the alcaide and warders came into his cell with lights bringing a suit of clothes, linen, best trousers, black striped with white. He was marched to join a couple of hundred other penitents squatted on the floor along the sides of a spacious gallery, all motionless but in an agony of apprehension, for none knew his doom. A large company of women were collected in a neighbouring chamber and a third lot in *sanbenitos,* among whom the priests moved seeking confessions and if made the boon of strangulation was conceded before " tasting the fire."

Shortly before sunrise the great bell of the Cathedral tolled and roused the city into life. People filled the chief streets, lined the thoroughfares and crowded into places whence they might best see the procession. With daylight Dellon saw from the faces of his companions that they were mostly Indians with but a dozen white men among them. M. Dellon went barefoot with the rest over the loose flints of the badly paved streets, and, at length, cut and bleeding, entered the church of St. Francisco, for the ceremony could not be performed under the fierce sky of this torrid climate. Dellon's punishment was confiscation of all his property, and banishment from India, with five years' service in the galleys of Portugal.

The rest of his sad adventures may be told briefly. He was brought back to Lisbon and worked at the oar with other convicts for some years, when at the intercession of friends in France the Portuguese government consented to release him. There is no record that the French authorities made any claim or reclamation for the ill-usage of a French subject.

It was otherwise with their neighbours, the Eng-

lish, who even before their power in India was established, would not suffer the Portuguese authorities in Goa to ill-treat a person who could claim
British protection. A French Capuchin, named
Father Ephrem, had visited Madras when on his
way to join the Catholic mission in Pegu. He was
invited to remain in Madras and was promised entire liberty with respect to his religion, and permitted to minister to the Catholics already settled in
the factory. In the course of his preaching he laid
down a dogma offensive, as it was asserted, to the
Mother of God, and information thereof was laid
with the inquisitors at Goa, who made their plans
to kidnap Father Ephrem and carry him off to Goa,
some six hundred miles distant from Madras. The
plot succeeded and the French Capuchin was lodged
in the prison of the Holy Office at Goa. This was
not to be brooked by the English in Madras. An
English ship forthwith proceeded to Goa and a
party of ten determined men, well-armed, landed
and appeared at the gates of the Inquisition and
demanded admittance. Leaving a couple of men on
guard at the gate, the rest entered the gaol and insisted at the point of the sword that Father Ephrem
should be forthwith surrendered to them. An order
thus enforced was irresistible, and the prisoner was
released, taken down to the ship's boat, reëmbarked
and carried back in safety to Madras.

The aims of the Inquisition are no longer those
of modern communities. So widely has the idea of

toleration extended, that we often forget how recent it is. The relations of Church and State are so changed in the last two centuries, that it is difficult to understand the times of the Spanish Inquisition. Then it was universally believed that orthodoxy in faith was intimately connected with loyalty to the state. As a matter of fact, nearly all the earlier heretical movements were also social or political revolts. It is, therefore, easy to see how heresy and high treason came to appear identical.

Some of the inquisitors were corrupt, others were naturally cruel, others, drunk with power, were more zealous in exerting that power than they were in deciding between guilt and innocence. On the other hand many were zealous because of their honesty. If a man believes that he knows the only hope of salvation, it is perfectly logical to compel another by force, if necessary, to follow that hope. Any physical punishment is slight compared with the great reward which reconciliation brings. On the other hand, if he is firm in his heresy, he is as dangerous as a wild beast. We are more tolerant now, less certain, perhaps, of our ground, but three or four hundred years ago these points were a stern reality.

That many inquisitors were more concerned with the Church as an institution than as a means of salvation is also true. They punished disrespect to an officer or to a law more severely than they did a doctrinal error, but that was, perhaps, inevitable. The Spanish Inquisition, which, as has been said, was to some extent a state affair, punished many for what we might call trifling offences, or, indeed, no offence at all, but it was an intolerant age, in and out of Spain.

The number punished has been grossly exaggerated, but it was enough to injure Spain permanently, to crush out freedom of thought and action to an unwarrantable extent. The historian must attribute much of Spain's decadence to the work of the mistaken advocate of absolute uniformity.

CHAPTER VI

EARLY PRISONS AND PRISONERS

Slow development of Prison Reform in Spain — Description
of the old Saladero — George Borrow's account of his arrest and imprisonment there — Balseiro's escape and subsequent escapades — He seizes the two sons of a wealthy
Basque and holds them for ransom — His capture and execution — The *valientes* or bullies — The cruelties they practised upon their weaker fellow prisoners — Don Rafael
Salillas' description of the Seville prison.

THE prisons in Spain have been generally divided
into three categories: First, the *depositos correcion-
ales,* the *carceles* or common gaols, one in the capital of each province, to which were sent accused persons and all sentenced to two years or less; second, the *presidios* of the Peninsula for convicts between two years and eight years; and third, the
African penal settlements for terms beyond eight
years. The character and condition of the bulk of
these places of durance long continued most unsat-
isfactory. In 1888 in an official report, the Minister of Grace and Justice said, " The present state of
the Spanish prisons is not enchanting. They are
neither safe nor wholesome, nor adapted to the ends
in view." This criticism was fully borne out by the

result of a general inquiry instituted. It was found that of a total of four hundred and fifty-six of the correctional prisons only one hundred and sixty-six were really fit for the purpose intended and the remainder were installed in any buildings available. Some were very ancient, dating back to the 16th century; and had once been palaces, religious houses, castles or fortresses.

Many of these buildings were ancient monuments which suffered much injury from the ignoble rôle to which they were put. A protest was published by a learned society of Madrid against the misuse of the superb ex-convents of San Gregorio in Valladolid and San Isidro del Campo near Seville, and the mutilation by its convict lodgers of the very beautiful gateway of the Templo de la Piedad in Guadalajara. The installation of the prison at Palma de Mallorca all but hopelessly impaired the magnificent cloisters of the convent of San Francisco, a thirteenth century architectural masterpiece, and a perfect specimen of the ogival form, like nothing else in Spain. Within a short period of ten years several of these interesting old buildings were ruined. The entire convent prison at Coruña sank, causing many casualties, loss of life and serious wounds.

Sometimes the authorities hired private dwellings to serve as prisons, or laid hands on whatever they could find. At Granada a slice of the Court House was used, a dark triangle to which air came only

from the interior yard. The prison of Allariz at
Orense was on the ground floor of a house in the
street, having two windows looking directly on to
it, guarded by a grating with bars so far apart that
a reasonably thin man could slip through. One of
the worst features of many of these ancient prisons
was their location in the very heart of the towns
with communication to the street. Friends gathered at the *rejas* outside, and the well known picture of flirtation at the prison window was drawn
from life. A common sight also was the out-
stretched hand of the starving prisoner imploring
alms from the charitable, for there was no regular
or sufficient supply of provisions within. Free access was also possible when the domestic needs of
the interior took the prisoners to the public well in
the street.

The Carmona gaol in Seville was for years half
in ruins; no sunlight reached any part of it with
the exception of two of the yards; the dungeons
had no ventilation except by a hole in their doors;
an open sewer ran through the gaol, the floors were
always wet, fleas abounded, as also rats, beetles and
cockroaches; cooking was done in one corner of the
exercising yard and clothes were washed in the
other. The removal of the gaol was ordered and
plans for a new building prepared in 1864, but they
were pigeon-holed until 1883, then sent back to be
revised, and the project is still delayed. The Col-
menar prison of Malaga was always under water

in heavy rain, and although simple repairs would have rectified this, nothing was done. The prison of Leon was condemned in 1878 as unfit for human habitation, and its alcalde (governor) stated that it had been reported for a century or more that it wanted light, air and sanitary arrangements; typhoid was endemic and three alcaldes had died of zymotic disease in a few years. It was generally denounced as " a poisonous pesthouse, a judicial burial ground." The Totana prison of Murcia was not properly a prison, but only a range of warehouses and shops fit for the storage of grain and herbs, but wholly unsuitable to lodge human beings. The district governor speaking of the Infiesto prison at Oviedo in 1853 wrote: " Humanity shudders at the horrible aspect of this detestable place."

At Cartagena the common gaol was on the ground floor of the *presidio* or convict prison. Here the innocent, still untried prisoners occupied a dark, damp den, enduring torments of discomfort, speedily losing health and strength, and exposed by its ruinous condition to the extremes of heat and cold in the varying seasons. Females were lodged on a lower floor, darker and closer and even exposed to the worst temptations. The convicts of the *presidio* had free access to their prison and immorality could not be prevented; no amount of supervision (and there was really none) could have checked the moral contamination more easily conveyed than the physical. These painful facts may be read in an official report dated October, 1877, and are practically the same as those detailed in the famous indictment of John Howard just a century earlier.[1]

Many of the makeshift prisons mentioned above were located in the very heart of towns and were without boundary walls or means of separation from the public, and two hundred and sixty-four had windows giving upon the streets. It was impossible to ensure safe custody so limited was the supervision, so insecure and ruinous the state of these imperfect prisons. Escapes had been of very frequent occurrence, but the total number could not be stated owing to the absence of accurate records from year to year. One authority gave the annual average of escapes as thirty-four, ranging over five successive years. They were greatly facilitated by the slack, slipshod system of discipline and the careless guard kept at the gates through which crowds constantly passed in and out. Friends admitted wholesale to visit prisoners brought in disguises and easily helped them to evade the vigilance of warders and keepers. Escapes were most numerous in the small gaols, — about three to one when compared to those from the *presidios*, — and were often effected on the way to gaol through the neglect or connivance of the escort, especially when the journey was made on foot and officers in charge willingly consented to linger on the road in order

[1] "Vida Penal en Espana," by Rafael Salillas, Madrid, 1888.

to enjoy themselves in the taverns and drinking shops. They even allowed their prisoners to pay lengthened visits to their own homes if situated anywhere near.

A famous escape took place, *en masse,* in one of the prisons on the occasion of a theatrical performance given by the prisoners in honour of the governor's birthday. Permission had been duly accorded and the function was organised on an imposing scale. The stage was erected in an open space, scenery provided and a fine curtain or act drop behind which the usual preparations were made. These had not gone beyond rehearsal, however. All was ready to " ring up," the prison audience all seated, enduring with increased impatience and dissatisfaction the long wait which seemed and was actually endless. At last the authorities interposed and the governor sent a messenger behind the curtain with a peremptory order to begin. There was no company. Every single soul, manager and actors had disappeared under cover of the curtain. A great hole or gap had been made in the outer wall, through which all of the performers had passed out to freedom.

Numerous as are the escapes, recaptures are also frequent. That fine corps, the *guardias civiles,* which constitutes the rural police of Spain, always so active in the prevention and suppression of crime, has been highly successful in the pursuit of fugitives, few of whom remain at large for any length of time. Travellers in Spain, especially in the country districts, must have been struck with the fine appearance of these stalwart champions of the law. They are all old soldiers, well trained and disciplined, ever on the side of order, never mixing in politics, and conspicuous for their loyalty to the existing régime.

The most disgraceful of the old prisons were in Madrid. The Saladero which survived until very recently had been once an abattoir and salting place of pigs. But it replaced one more ancient and even worse in every aspect. The earlier construction is described by a Spanish writer, Don Francisco Lastres, as the most meagre, the darkest, dirtiest place imaginable. It had yet a deeper depth, an underground dungeon, commonly called "el Infierno," hell itself, in which light was so scarce that when new comers arrived, the old occupants could only make out their faces by striking matches, manufactured from scraps of linen steeped in grease saved from their soup or salad oil. When the gaol was emptied it was so encrusted with abominable filth that to clean it was out of the question and the whole place was swept bodily out of existence.

This must have been the prison in which George Borrow was confined when that enterprising Englishman was arrested for endeavouring to circulate the Bible in Spain, as the agent and representative of the British Bible Society in 1835 and the following years. His experiences as told by himself con-stitute one of the most thrilling books of adventure in the English language, and his strangely interesting personality will long be remembered and admired. He had led a very varied life, had wandered the world over as the friend and associate of those curious people, the gipsies, whose " crabbed " language he spoke with fluency and to whose ways and customs he readily conformed. Readers whom his " Lavengro " and " The Romany Rye " have delighted will bear witness to the daring and intrepid character which carried him safely through many difficult and dangerous situations. He was a man of great stature, well trained in the art of self defence, as he proved by his successful contest with the " Flaming Tinker " described in " Lavengro." The bigoted Spanish authorities caught a Tartar in Borrow. It was easy to arrest him as he was nothing loth to go to gaol; he had long been thinking, as he tells us, " of paying a visit to the prison, partly in the hope of being able to say a few words of Christian instruction to the criminals and partly with a view to making certain investigations in the robber language of Spain." But, once in, he refused to come out. He took high ground; his arrest had been unlawful; he had never been tried or condemned and nothing would satisfy him but a full and complete apology from the Spanish government. He was strongly backed up by the British Ambassador and he was gratified in the end by the almost abject surrender of the authorities.

But he spent three weeks within the walls and we have to thank his indomitable spirit for a glimpse into the gloomy recesses of the Carcel de la Corte, the chief prison, at that time, of the capital of Spain.

The arrest was made openly in one of the principal streets of Madrid by a couple of *alguazils* who carried their prisoner to the office of the *corregidor,* or chief magistrate, where he was abruptly informed that he was to be forthwith committed to gaol. He was led across the Plaza Mayor, the great square so often the scene in times past of the *autos da fé.* Borrow, as he went, cast his eyes at the balcony of the city hall where, on one occasion, " the last of the Austrian line in Spain (Philip II) sat, and, after some thirty heretics of both sexes had been burnt by fours and fives, wiped his face perspiring with heat and black with smoke and calmly inquired, ' *No hay mas?* ' " (No more to come?) for which exemplary proof of patience he was much applauded by his priests and confessors, who subsequently poisoned him.

" We arrived at the prison," Borrow goes on, " which stands in a narrow street not far from the great square. We entered a dusty passage at the end of which was a wicket. There was an exchange of words and in a few moments I found myself within the prison of Madrid, in a kind of corridor which overlooked at a considerable altitude what appeared to be a court from which arose a hubbub of voices and occasional wild shouts and cries. . . ." Several people sat here, one of whom received the warrant of committal, perused it with attention and, rising, advanced towards Borrow.

"What a figure! He was about forty years of age and . . . in height might have been some six feet two inches had his body not been curved much after the fashion of the letter S. No weasel ever appeared lanker; his face might have been called handsome, had it not been for his extraordinary and portentous meagreness; his nose was like an eagle's bill, his teeth white as ivory, his eyes black (oh, how black!) and fraught with a strange expression; his skin was dark and the hair of his head like the plumage of a raven. A deep quiet smile dwelt continually on his features, but with all the quiet it was a cruel smile, such a one as would have graced the countenance of a Nero.

"'Caballero,' he said, 'allow me to introduce myself as the alcaide of this prison. . . . I am to have the honour of your company for a time, a short time doubtless, beneath this roof; I hope you will banish every apprehension from your mind. I am charged to treat you with all respect, a needless charge and Cabellero, you will rather consider yourself here as a guest than as a prisoner. Pray issue whatever commands you may think fit to the turn-keys and officials as if they were your own servants. I will now conduct you to your apartment. We invariably reserve it for cavaliers of distinction.

No charge will be made for it although the daily hire is not unfrequently an ounce of gold.'

" This speech was delivered in pure sonorous Castilian with calmness, gravity and almost dignity and would have done honour to a gentleman of high birth. Now, who in the name of wonder, was this alcaide? One of the greatest rascals in all Spain. A fellow who more than once by his grasping cupidity and his curtailment of the miserable rations of the prisoners caused an insurrection in the court below only to be repressed by bloodshed and the summoning of military aid; a fellow of low birth who five years previously had been a drummer to a band of Royalist volunteers."

The room allotted to Borrow was large and lofty, but totally destitute of any kind of furniture except a huge wooden pitcher containing the day's allowance of water. But no objection was made to Borrow's providing for himself and a messenger was forthwith despatched to his lodgings to fetch bed and bedding and all necessaries, with which came a supply of food, and the new prisoner soon made himself fairly comfortable. He ate heartily, slept soundly and rejoiced next day to hear that this illegal arrest and confinement of a British subject was already causing the high-handed minister who had ordered it, much uneasiness and embarrassment. Borrow steadfastly refused to go free without full and ample reparation for the violence and injustice done to him. " Take notice," he declared, "that I will not quit this prison till I have received full satisfaction for having been sent hither uncondemned. You may expel me if you please, but any attempt to do so shall be resisted with all the bodily strength of which I am possessed." In the end the *amende* was made in an official document admitting that he had been imprisoned on insufficient grounds, and Borrow went out after three weeks' incarceration, during which he learned much concerning the prison and the people it contained.

He refrains from a particular description of the place. "It would be impossible," he says, "to describe so irregular and rambling an edifice. Its principal features consisted of two courts, the one behind the other, in which the great body of the prisoners took air and recreation. Three large vaulted dungeons or *calabozos* occupied the three sides of the (first) court . . . roomy enough to contain respectively from one hundred to one hundred and fifty prisoners who were at night secured with lock and bar, but during the day were permitted to roam about the courts as they thought fit. The second court was considerably larger than the first, though it contained but two dungeons, horribly filthy and disgusting, used for the reception of the lower grades of thieves. Of the two dungeons one was if possible yet more horrible than the other. It was called the *gallinería* or 'chicken coop' because within it every night were pent up the young fry of the prison, wretched boys from seven to fifteen years of age, the greater part almost in a state of nudity. The common bed of all the inmates of these dungeons was the ground, between which and their bodies nothing intervened save occasionally a *manta* or horse cloth or perhaps a small mattress; this latter luxury was however of exceedingly rare occurrence.

"Besides the *calabozos* connected with the courts were other dungeons in various parts of the prison, some of them quite dark, intended for the reception of those whom it might be deemed expedient to treat with peculiar severity. There was likewise a ward set apart for females. Connected with the principal corridor were many small apartments where resided prisoners confined for debt or for political offences, and, lastly, there was a small *capilla* or chapel in which prisoners cast for death passed the last three days of their existence in the company of their ghostly advisers.

"I shall not forget my first Sunday in prison. Sunday is the gala day . . . and whatever robber finery is to be found in it is sure to be exhibited on that day of holiness. There is not a set of people in the world more vain than robbers in general, more fond of cutting a figure whenever they have an opportunity. The famous Jack Sheppard delighted in sporting a suit of Genoese velvet and when he appeared in public generally wore a silver hilted sword by his side. . . . Many of the Italian

bandits go splendidly decorated, the cap alone of
the Haram Pacha, the head of the cannibal gipsy
band which infested Hungary at the conclusion of
the 18th century, was adorned with gold and jewels
to the value of several thousand guilders. . . .
The Spanish robbers are as fond of display as their
brethren of other lands, and whether in prison or
out are never so happy as when decked out in a
profusion of white linen in which they can loll in
the sun or walk jauntily up and down."

To this day, snow-white linen is an especial mark
of foppery in the Spanish peasant. To put on a
clean shirt is considered a sufficient and satisfactory
substitute for a bath and in the humblest house a
white table cloth is provided for meals and clean
sheets for the beds. Borrow gives a graphic picture
of the " tip-top thieves " he came across. " Neither
coat nor jacket was worn over the shirt, the sleeves
of which were wide and flowing, only a waistcoat
of green or blue silk with an abundance of silver
buttons which are intended more for show than
use, as the waistcoat is seldom buttoned. Then
there are wide trousers something after the Turk-
ish fashion; around the waist is a crimson *faja* or
girdle and about the head is tied a gaudily coloured
handkerchief from the loom of Barcelona. Light
pumps and silk stockings complete the robber's
array.

" Amongst those who particularly attracted my
attention were a father and son; the former a tall

athletic figure, of about thirty, by profession a housebreaker and celebrated through Madrid for the peculiar dexterity he exhibited in his calling. He was in prison for an atrocious murder committed in the dead of night in a house in Caraban-chel (a suburb of Madrid), in which his only accomplice was his son, a child under seven years of age. The imp was in every respect the counterpart of his father though in miniature. He too wore the robber shirt sleeves, the robber waistcoat with the silver buttons, the robber kerchief round his brow and, ridiculously enough, a long Manchegan knife in the crimson faja. He was evidently the pride of the ruffian father who took all imaginable care of him, would dandle him on his knee, and would occasionally take the cigar from his own mustachioed lips and insert it in the urchin's mouth. The boy was the pet of the court, for the father was one of the 'bullies' of the prison and those who feared his prowess and wished to pay their court to him were always fondling the child."

Borrow when in the " Carcel de la Corte " re-newed his acquaintance with one, Balseiro, whom he had met in a low tavern frequented by thieves and bull fighters on a previous visit to Madrid. One of these, Sevilla by name, professed deep admiration for the Englishman and backed him to know more than most people of the " crabbed " Gitano language. A match was made with this Balseiro who claimed to have been in prison half

his life and to be on most intimate terms with the
gipsies. When Borrow came across him for the
second time he was confined in an upper story of
the prison in a strong room with other malefactors.
There was no mistaking this champion criminal
with his small, slight, active figure and his handsome features, " but they were those of a demon."
He had recently been found guilty of aiding and
abetting a celebrated thief, Pepe Candelas, in a desperate robbery perpetrated in open daylight on no
less a person than the Queen's milliner, a French-
woman, whom they bound in her own shop, from
which they took goods to the amount of five or six
thousand dollars. Candelas had already suffered
for his crime, but Balseiro, whose reputation was
the worse of the two, had saved his life by the plentiful use of money, and the capital sentence had in
his case been commuted to twenty years' hard labour
in the *presidio* of Malaga.

When Borrow condoled with him, Balseiro
laughed it off, saying that within a few weeks he
would be transferred and could at any time escape
by bribing his guards. But he was not content to
wait and joined with several fellow convicts who
succeeded in breaking through the roof of the prison
and getting away. He returned forthwith to his
evil courses and soon committed a number of fresh
and very daring robberies in and around Madrid.
At length dissatisfied with the meagre results and
the smallness of the plunder he secured, Balseiro

planned a great stroke to provide himself with sufficient funds to leave the country and live elsewhere in luxurious idleness.

A Basque named Gabira, a man of great wealth, held the post of comptroller of the Queen's household. He had two sons, handsome boys of twelve and fourteen years of age respectively, who were being educated at a school in Madrid. Balseiro, well aware of the father's strong affection for his children, resolved to make it subservient to his rapacity. He planned to carry off the boys and hold them for ransom at an enormous price. Two of his confederates, well-dressed and of respectable appearance, drove up to the school and presenting a forged letter, purporting to be written by the father, persuaded the schoolmaster to let them go out for a jaunt in the country. They were carried off to a hiding place of Balseiro's in a cave some five miles from Madrid in a wild unfrequented spot between the Escorial and the village of Torre Lodones. Here the two children were sequestered in the safekeeping of their captors, while Balseiro remained in Madrid to conduct negotiations with the bereaved father. But Gabira was a man of great energy and determination and altogether declined to agree to the terms proposed. He invoked the power of the authorities instead, and, at his request, parties of horse and foot soldiers were sent to scour the country and the cave was soon discovered, with the children, who had been deserted by their guards in terror at the news of the rigorous search instituted. Further search secured the capture of the accomplices and they were identified by their young victims. Balseiro, when his part in the plot became known, fled from the capital but was speedily caught, tried, and with his associates suffered death on the scaffold. Gabira with his two children was present at the execution.

A brief description of the old Saladero, which has at last disappeared off the face of the earth, may be of interest. It stood at the top of the Santa Barbara hill on the left hand side, in external aspect a half-ruined edifice tottering to its fall, propped and buttressed, at one corner quite past mending, at another showing rotten cement and plaster with its aged weather-worn walls stained with great black patches of moisture and decay. A poor and wretched place outside with no architectural pretensions, its interior was infinitely worse. It was entered by a wide entrance not unlike that of an ancient country inn or hostelry with a broken-down wooden staircase, leading to a battered doorway of rotten timbers. The portals passed, the prison itself was reached, a series of underground cellars with vaulted roofs purposely constructed, as it seemed, to exclude light and prevent ventilation, permeated constantly with fetid odours and abominable foul exhalations from the perpetual want of change of atmosphere or circulation of fresh air. Yet human beings were left to rot in these nauseous and pestif-

erous holes for two or three years continuously.
At times the detention lasted five years on account
of the disgracefully slow procedure in the law courts
and this although trials often ended in acquittal or
a verdict of non-responsibility for the criminal act
charged. Many of the unfortunate wretches subjected to these interminable delays and waiting
judgment, therefore still innocent in the eyes of
the law, were yet herded with those already convicted of the most heinous offences.

This neglect of the rules, generally accepted as
binding upon civilised governments in the treatment
of those whom the law lays by the heels, produced
deplorable results. The gaol fever, that ancient
scourge which once ravaged ill-kept prisons and
swept away thousands, but long ago eliminated
from proper places of durance, survived in the Saladero of Madrid until quite a recent date. Forty
cases occurred as late as 1876 and zymotic disease
was endemic in the prison. It was also a hotbed of
vice, where indiscriminate association of all categories, good, bad and indifferent — the worst always in the ascendent, fostered and developed criminal instincts and multiplied criminals of the most
daring and accomplished kind. When, with a storm
of indignant eloquence, an eminent Spanish deputy,
Don Manuel Silvela, denounced the Saladero in
the Cortes and took the lead in insisting upon its
demolition, he pointed out its many shortcomings.
It was in the last degree unhealthy; it was nearly

useless as a place of detention, for the bold or ingenious prisoner laughed at its restraints and escapes took place daily to the number of fourteen and sixteen at a time. If, however, with increased precautions it was possible to keep prisoners secure within the walls, nothing could save them from one another. Contamination was widespread and unceasing in a mass of men left entirely to themselves without regular occupation, without industrial labour or improving education and with no outlet for their energies but demoralising talk and vicious practices. Not strangely the Saladero became a great criminal centre, a workshop and manufactory of false money, where strange frauds were devised, such as the *entierro* [1] or suggested revelation of hidden treasure, the well known Spanish swindle which has had ramifications almost all over the world.

'An independent witness, nevertheless, speaking from experience, the same George Borrow already quoted, has a good word to say for the inmates of Spanish gaols. He was greatly surprised at their orderly conduct and quiet demeanour. " They had their occasional bursts of wild gaiety; their occasional quarrels which they were in the habit of settling in a corner of the interior court with their long knives, the result not infrequently being death or a dreadful gash in the face or abdomen; but upon the whole their conduct was infinitely superior to

[1] See *post*, p. 161.

what might have been expected from the inmates
of such a place. Yet this was not the result of coercion or any particular care which was exercised
over them; for perhaps in no part of the world are
prisoners so left to themselves and so utterly neglected as in Spain, the authorities having no further
anxiety about them than to prevent their escape,
not the slightest attention being paid to their moral
conduct, — not a thought bestowed on their health,
comfort or mental improvement whilst within the
walls. Yet in this prison of Madrid, and I may say
in Spanish prisons in general (for I have been an
inmate of more than one), the ears of the visitor
are never shocked with horrid blasphemy and obscenity as in those of some other countries and
more particularly in civilised France, nor are his
eyes outraged or himself insulted as he would as-
suredly be were he to look down upon the courts
from the galleries of the Bicêtre (in Paris)." And
yet in this prison of Madrid were some of the most
desperate characters in Spain; ruffians who had
committed acts of cruelty and atrocity sufficient to
make one shudder with horror. Gravity and se-
dateness are the leading characteristics of the Spaniards, and the worst robber, except in those moments
when he is engaged in his occupation, (and then no
one is more sanguinary, pitiless and wolfishly eager
for booty), is a being who can be courteous and affable and who takes pleasure in conducting himself
with sobriety and decorum. Borrow thought so

well of these fellow-prisoners that he was willing
to entertain them at dinner in his own private apartment in the gaol, and the governor made no objection to knocking off their irons temporarily so that
they might enjoy the meal in comfort and convenience.

A more intimate acquaintance with the inner life
of the Spanish gaols has been accorded by a modern
writer, Don Rafael Salillas. He summarises all its
evils in the single word "money." All disorders
and shortcomings, the corruption, the absence of
discipline, the cruelties perpetrated, the prevailing
license, the shameful immorality constantly winked
at or openly permitted, have had one and the same
origin, the use and misuse of the private funds the
prisoners have at their disposal. Until quite a recent date, everything, even temporary liberty, had
its price in Spanish prisons. This vicious system
dated from the times when the "alcaide" or head
of an establishment, the primary purpose of which
was the safe custody of offenders, bought his place
and was permitted to recoup himself as best he
could out of his charges. The same abominable
practice was at one time almost a world-wide practice, but nowhere has it flourished so largely as in
Spain. No attempt was made to check it; it was
acknowledged and practically deemed lawful.

In an ancient work on the prison of Seville, dating
from the sixteenth century, the writer, Christobal
de Chaves, classifies the interior under three heads;

the spaces entered respectively by three doors of gold, silver or copper, each metal corresponding to the profits drawn from each. Imprisonment might be made more tolerable by payment regulated according to a fixed tariff. For a certain sum any prisoner might go home to sleep, he might purchase food where little, if any, was provided, he might escape fetters or purchase " easement of irons," as in the old English prisons. To enhance the value of the relief afforded worse hardships were inflicted at the outset. Restraint was made most irksome in the beginning of imprisonment. The fetters were then the heaviest and most varied, the deepest and vilest dungeons were the first quarters allotted. A plain hint of relaxation and alleviation was given, to be obtained at a price and the converse made equally certain. Increased pain and discomfort were the penalty for those who would not, or, worse still, who could not produce the extortionate sums demanded. Tasks imposed were rendered more difficult; it was a common practice to oil or grease the rope by which water was raised from a well, so that it should slip through the fingers and intensify the labour.

When authority had sold its good will or wrung the life blood from its victims they were handed over to the tender mercies of their fellow prisoners, the self-constituted masters and irresponsible tyrants in the place. The most brutal and overbearing ruled supreme within the walls and levied taxes by the

right of the strongest. The "garnish" of the old
British prisons, the enforced payments to gain a first
footing, was exacted to the last in Spain from all
new arrivals and was called " *cobrar el patente*," *i. e.*
collecting the dues. To hesitate or refuse payment
was promptly punished by cruel blows; the default-
ers were flogged; they got the *culebrazo* (whipping) with a rope kept for the purpose. The quite
penniless were despoiled of their clothing and con-
soled with the remark that it was better for them
to take to their beds because they were naked, than
on account of injuries and wounds, or they wrapped
themselves up in some ragged cloak infested with
fleas. The bullies or *valientes* were not interfered
with by the authorities but rather supported by
them. In fact they played into each other's hands.
Both worked their wicked will upon their victims
and in their own way, — the authorities by right of
the legal powers they wielded, the master-prison-
ers by force of character and the strength of their
muscles. Both squeezed out money like juice from
a lemon, robbed, swindled or stole all that came in
their way.

Guzman de Alfarache, the typical thief of the
time of Philip II, whose life and adventures are told
by the author of the most famous of the picaresque
novels, describes his journey from Seville to Cadiz
to embark upon one of the galleys which made up
the naval power of Spain. "As we started on the
road, we came upon a swine-herd with a number of

young pigs, which we surrounded and captured, each
of us taking one. The man howled to our commissary that he should make us restore them, but he
turned a deaf ear and we stuck to our plunder. At
the first halt we laid hands on other goods and concealed them inside one of the pigs when the commissary interposed, discovered the things and took possession of them himself."

The alcaide of the prison turned everything to
profit. He sold the Government stores, bedding
and clothing to the prison bullies who retailed the
pieces to individual prisoners. He trafficked in the
disciplinary processes, accepting bribes to overlook
misconduct, and pandered to the worst vices of the
inmates by allowing visitors of both sexes to have
free access to them and to bring in all manner of
prohibited articles, unlimited drink, and dangerous
weapons, knives and daggers and other arms for
use in attack and defence in the quarrels and murderous conflicts continually occurring.

A fruitful source of profit was the sale of privi-
leged offices, permits to hawk goods and to trade
within the precincts of the prison. Salillas when he
visited the Seville prison not many years ago, saw
numbers of prisoners selling cigars and cigarettes in
the yards, various articles of food, such as *gaz-
pacho,* the popular salad of Andalusia, compounded
of oil and bread soaked in water, and drinks including *aguardiente,* that powerful Spanish spirit akin
to Hollands. Some kept gaming tables and paid a

tax on each game and its profits and especially
when the " King " was turned up at " Monte."

Salillas publishes a list of prices that ruled for
places, privileges and boons conceded to the prisoners. To become a " *cabo de vara*," a " corporal carrying the stick " or wand of office, cost from eight
to sixteen dollars. " Who and what was the *Cabo
de Vara?* " he asks and answers the question. " A
hybrid creature the offspring of such diverse parents as the law and crime; half murderer, half
robber, who after living in defiance of the law is at
least prevented from doing further harm in freedom,
is locked up and entrusted with executive authority
over companions who have passed through the same
evil conditions and are now at his mercy. He is
half galley-slave chained to the oar, half public
functionary wearing the badge of officialdom and
armed with a stick to enforce his authority. He
represents two very opposite sets of ideas; on the
one hand that of good order and the maintenance
of penal discipline, on the other that of a natural
inclination towards the wrong doing in which he has
been a practitioner and for which he is, in a way,
enduring the penalty. To succeed he must possess
some strongly marked personal qualities; he should
be able to bully and impose his will upon those
subjected to his influence, overbearing, masterful,
swaggering, ready to take the law into his own
hands and insist upon its observance as he chooses
to interpret its dictates."

The post of hospital orderly or cook or laundry-man could be secured for about the same price, while a small fee to the prison surgeon gained a perfectly sound man admission to hospital for treatment he did not need, but in which he was much more comfortable than in the ordinary prison. The place of prison barber was to be bought for four dollars; employment as a shoemaker two dollars; relief from a punishment ordered three dollars; permission to pay a visit home, four dollars. These prices were not definitely settled and unchangeable. Where a certain profit could be extracted from a particular post such as the charge of the canteen it was put up to auction and knocked down to the highest bidder.

CHAPTER VII

PRESIDIOS AT HOME AND ABROAD

The presidio or convict prison — Stations at home and in
Northern Africa — Convict labour — Cruelties inflicted on
the presidiarios employed in road making — Severity of the
régime at Valladolid — Evils of overcrowding — Ceuta —
Its fortifications — Early history — The *entierro* or "Spanish swindle" — Several interesting instances — Monsignor
X — Armand Carron — M. Elked — Credulity of the victims — Boldness of the swindlers — Attempt to dupe a
Yorkshire squire — Discovery of the fraud.

THE Spanish " presidios " or penal establishments
for offenders sentenced to long terms are the counterpart of the English convict prisons. They are of
two classes, those at home in provincial capitals or
in fortresses and strongholds, and those abroad installed in North Africa, as the alternative or substitute for the penal colonies beyond the sea established
by Italy and France. Home presidios are at Burgos,
Cartagena, Granada, Ocana, Santona, Valladolid
and Saragossa. There are two at Valencia, one at
Tarragona and two more at Alcala de Henares. Of
the foregoing that of Cartagena was especially constructed to meet the needs of the arsenal and dock-
yard and is spoken of as deplorably deficient by

those who visited it. Four hundred convicts were
lodged miserably in one dormitory; their bedding
consisted of a rough mattress and one brown rug;
clothing was issued only every two years; the die-
taries were supplied by a thievish contractor who
supplied a soup consisting of beans boiled in water,
abstracting the ration of oil and bacon. A presidio
of ancient date was installed in the arsenal of La
Carraca near Cadiz, a survival really of the *galera*
or galleys planted on shore when human motive
power ceased to be used in propelling warships.

A terrible story is preserved of the cruelties inflicted on a number of these *presidiarios* employed
to make the road between San Lucar de Barrameda
and Puerto Santa Maria. Their labour was leased
to an inhuman contractor who worked them literally to death. They were half-starved, over-bur-
thened with chains and continually flogged so that
within one year half their whole number of one
thousand had disappeared; they had died " of pri-
vation, of blows, hunger, cold, insufficient clothing
and continuous neglect." The contractor cleared a
large profit, but lost it and died in extreme poverty
after having been arraigned and tried for his life
as a murderer.

The presidio of Valladolid was also condemned
for the severity of its régime. The climate alter-
nated between great summer heat and extreme cold
in winter, but the convicts worked in the quarries
in all weathers. The death record rose in this prison

to such a high figure that a third of the average
total population of three thousand perished within
eighteen months. The general average of the presidios was low but as a rule the death rate was not
high. Even when twenty per cent. of males and
twenty-five per cent. of the females were sick and
hospital accommodation was scarce and imperfect,
the deaths did not exceed two and a half per cent.
per annum and this included the fatal results of
quarrels ending in duels to the death. One of the
most serious evils was overcrowding. Official figures give the prison population as about nineteen
thousand and the available house-room was for not
more than twelve thousand. Salillas puts it at a
much lower total, asserting there was barely room
for three thousand.

While the prisons of Cuba are not strictly within
the scope of this work, one of historic and particular
interest may be mentioned. This is Morro Castle,
which still guards the Harbour of Havana. It was
begun in 1589, soon after the unsuccessful attack on
Havana by Drake, and was finished in 1597. In
1862 it was partly destroyed by the English who
captured it and remained in possession of the city
for a year. The arms of the city, granted by royal
decree, were appropriately three castles of silver on
a blue field, and a golden key. The castles were
La Fuerza, El Morro and La Punta, guarding the
harbour.

The ancient fortress has been described as a

"great mass of dun coloured rock and tower and battlement and steep, of which the various parts seem to have grown into one another." It contains cells as damp, dark and unwholesome as those in the notorious dungeons of the old world. This is testified to by a California journalist, Charles Michelson, who was arrested by mistake and thrown into a cell in the castle just before the Spanish-American War. Although he was liberated in two days, his experience was not soon forgotten. The cell was an arch of heavy masonry, damp with the moisture of years. The only window was high up in the arch, and there was no furniture — no bed, blanket or chair. He was not without company of a kind, however, for the place was full of cockroaches and rats. When he clambered up and tried to look out of the window, which commands a fine view of the harbour, a guard outside poked at him with a bayonet. The soup brought him was, he said, "strong and scummy, and the can had been so recently emptied of its original contents that there was a film of oil over the top of it." His interpreter, who was arrested at the same time, fared worse, for he was bound and kept in even a fouler cell.

In the days of Spanish sovereignty, many Cuban prisoners were shot and their bodies were hurled from the outer wall of the castle to the sharks of the so-called "shark's nest," forty feet below, on the gulf side.

There are said to be many caverns in the castle

through which the rush and noise of the waves make music, but this is probably due to the winds rather than the tides.

Spain maintains several presidios beyond sea, chiefly on the North African coast, and there is one also at Palma de Mallorca, one of the Balearic islands. Those in Africa are Alhucemas, Melilla, Peñon de Velez de la Gomera, Chaferinas and Ceuta, immediately opposite Gibraltar, which is no doubt the first and original of all Spanish presidios. The expression when first used was taken to convey the meaning of a penal settlement, established within a fortress under military rule and guardianship, with its personnel constantly employed on the fortifications, constructing, repairing and making good wear and tear, and answering, if need be, the call to arms in reinforcement of the regular garrison. The early records of Ceuta prove this. This stronghold, on one side rising out of the sea, with its landward defences ever confronting a fierce hostile power, was exposed at all times to siege and incursion. When the Moorish warriors became too bold the Spanish general sallied forth to beat up their quarters, destroy their batteries and drive them back into the mountains. Working parties of *presidiarios,* armed, accompanied the troops and did excellent service, eager, as the old chronicler puts it, to clear their characters by their heroism, " always supposing that blood may wash out crime."

Ceuta was a type of the military colony beyond

sea, held by a strong garrison against warlike natives who resisted the invasion and would have
driven out the intruders. The settlement was secured by continual fortification in which the abundant penal labour was constantly employed. Its
social conditions were precisely similar to those
which obtained in the early days of Australian trans-
portation and such as prevail to-day in the French
penal colony of New Caledonia. The population is
made up of two principal classes, bond and free.
The first are convicts serving their sentences and the
second the officials who guard them. Ordinary
colonists have not settled to any large extent in
these North African possessions. A few traders
and agriculturists have come seeking such fortune
as offers and the number of residents is increased by
released convicts, the counterpart of the emancipist
class in the Antipodes, who remain with the pros-
pect of earning a livelihood honestly, instead of
lapsing into evil courses on their return to the
mother country.

Ceuta is essentially a convict city, not exactly
founded by penal labour but enlarged and improved
by it and served by it in all the needs of daily domestic life. The first period of close confinement on
arrival is comparatively brief and is spent in the
prison proper outside the city at hard labour in
association on the fortifications, in the workshops
and quarries. In the second period the convicts are
permitted to enter the city and are employed under

supervision in warehouses, offices and in water carrying. In the third period, commonly called from "gun to gun," extending daily from the morning gun fire until the evening, the convicts are allowed to go freely into the city and work there on their own account. The fourth and last, entered when two thirds of the whole sentence has been completed, is called "under conditions," that is to say, in conditional freedom, and the convicts are let out to private employers precisely as they were "assigned" in old Australian days. They may live with their masters, sleep out, and are only obliged to report at the prison once a month for muster. More than a third of the total number are thus employed.

The result is that Ceuta offers the singular spectacle that it is nominally a prison, but the bulk of the prisoners live beyond the walls, quite unguarded and really in the streets forming part of the ordinary population. Convicts are to be met with at every corner, they go in and out through the front doors of houses, no one looks at them in surprise, no one draws aside to let them pass. The situation is described graphically by Salillas. "Who is the coachman on the box? A convict. Who is the man who waits at table? A convict. The cook in the kitchen? A convict. The nursemaid in charge of the children? A convict (male). Are their employers afraid of being robbed or murdered? Not in the least."

Another eye witness [1] writes : —

" Could this happen in any other city in Spain? If the inhabitants found themselves rubbing shoulders with the scum of the earth, with the worst malefactors, with criminals guilty of the most heinous offences, would they have enjoyed one moment's peace? Could they overcome the natural repugnance felt by honest and respectable people for those whom the law has condemned to live apart? The fact is that at Ceuta no one objects. The existing state of things is deemed the most natural thing in the world. It has been too long the rule and it is claimed seriously that no evil consequences have resulted. The utmost confidence is reposed in these ex-criminals whose nature has been seemingly quite changed by relegation to the African presidio. They wash and get up linen without losing more pieces than a first class washerwoman, they wait on the children with the tenderest concern, they perform all sorts of household service, go to market, run messages, polish the floors and the furniture with all the zeal and industry of the best servants in the world. The most cordial relations exist between employers and their convict attendants and cases have been known where the former have carried the latter back to Spain to continue their service. One was a Chinese cook who was excused ten years' supervision to go back with his master."

It is claimed by the champions of Ceuta that

[1] Relosillas, "Four Months in Ceuta."

despite the freedom accorded to the convicts their
conduct is exemplary. "I can certify," says Relosillas [1] "that during a whole year there were but
three or four instances of crime amongst the convicts employed in domestic service." Others however are not so laudatory. An independent witness,
Doña Concepcion Arenal, has little good to say of
the prisons. "In them justice is punished or rather
crucified," she wrote, "and with it hygiene, morality, decency, humanity, all, in a word, which every
one who is not himself hateful and contemptible,
respects. It is impossible to give any idea of the
cuartel principal or chief convict barrack in the
place. We can only refer to its terrible and revolting demoralisation." Yet she is inclined to contradict herself and argues that the convict when trusted
will behave well. His life on the whole is light and
easy; he has sufficient food, congenial company, and
can better his position by steady industry; he wears
no chains, performs no rude or laborious tasks and
is driven neither into insubordination nor crime.

The statements just quoted are hardly credible
and cannot be reconciled with the reports of others,
from personal experience. Mr. Cook, an English
evangelist, who has devoted himself to extensive
prison visitation, has drawn a dark picture of this
ideal penal settlement as he saw it in 1892. At that
date general idleness was the rule. Hundreds hung
about with no work to do. Criminals with the

[1] "Four Months in Ceuta."

worst antecedents were included in the prison population. One had been a *bandido* or brigand who had been guilty of seven murders; another had four murders to his credit and one assassin was in a totally dark cell, confined hand and foot, condemned to death and daily expecting to be shot. No fewer than one hundred and twelve slept in one large room without more supervision than that exercised by their fellows discharging the functions of warders. Mr. Cook expresses his wonder that they did not break out oftener into rebellion. As a matter of fact and as against the statement given above, outbreaks were not uncommon with fierce attacks upon officers and murderous affrays among the prisoners. Crime and misconduct are certainly not unknown in Ceuta.

A gruesome description was given by a correspondent writing to the *London Times* in the year 1876. When he visited the citadel prison he found from eight hundred to one thousand convicts lodged there in a wretched condition, clad only in tattered rags, the cast off uniforms of soldiers, generally insufficient for decency. They tottered in and out of the ruinous sheds supposed to shelter them, quarrelled like hyenas over their meagre and repulsive rations, which were always short through the dishonesty of the thieving contractor, and fought to the death with the knives which every one carried. Each shed contained from one to two hundred where they lay like beasts upon the ground. Vermin

crept up the wall and dirt abounded on all sides.
" No words of mine," said this outspoken eye-witness, " can paint the darkness, the filth, the seething
corruption of these dens of convicts, dens into which
no streak of sunlight, divine or human, ever finds
its way, and where nothing is seen or heard but outrage and cruelty on the one hand, misery and star-
vation and obscenity on the other." There was a
worse place, the " Presidio del Campo," or field
prison in which the hard labour gangs [1] employed
on the fortifications were housed in still filthier
hovels, with less food and more demoralisation.
This same correspondent when he enquired his way
to the presidio was told by a Spanish officer : " They
are not presidios but the haunts of wild beasts and
nurseries of thieves." Obviously there is much dis-
crepancy in the various accounts published.

The true state of the case may best be judged by
examining and setting forth the conditions prevailing. On the surface the convicts may seem to abstain from serious misconduct, but even this may be
doubted from the facts in evidence. " It is a wild
beasts' cage," writes one well informed authority.
It may be to some extent a cage without bars, or in
which the wild beasts are so tamed that they may
be allowed to go at large and do but little harm, but

---

[1] Irons are not carried by the convicts, not even by those
sentenced to imprisonment "in chains," *con la cadena*. They
were considered an interference with the efforts and strength
of the labourer.

evil instincts are at times in the ascendancy as
shown in the quarrels and disorders that occur, but
to no greater extent says the apologist than in any
of the prisons on the Spanish mainland. It may be
that the régime is so mild that the convicts yield
willingly to it without a murmur and seldom rise
against it. But the very atmosphere of the place is
criminal. There may be few prison offences where
rules are easy but if serious offences against discipline are but rarely committed within the limits,
others against society are constantly prepared for
execution beyond. Ceuta is a hot bed of crime, the
seed is sown there, nourished and developed to bear
baleful fruit afterwards. It is a first class school for
the education of thieves, swindlers, coiners, and for-
gers who graduate and take honours in the open
world of evil doing. It is the original home, some
say, of the famous fraud, peculiarly Spanish, called
the *entierro,* which still flourishes and draws profit
as ever, not from Spain alone, but from far and
wide in nearly all civilised countries.

The *entierro,* or the " burial " literally translated,
means an artful and specious proposal to reveal
the whereabouts of a buried treasure. It is another
form of the well known " confidence trick " or, as the
French call it, the " *vol a l'americaine,*" and we cannot but admire the ingenuity and inventiveness so
often displayed in its practice, while expressing surprise at the credulity and gullibility of those who are
deluded by it. It originates as a rule in a letter ad-

dressed from the prison to some prominent person in Spain or elsewhere, for the astute practitioner is well provided with lists of names likely to be useful to him in his business. It is on record that a seizure was made in the presidio of Granada of a whole stock in trade, a great mass of information secretly collected from all parts of the world to serve in carrying out the fraud of the *entierro,* and with it a number of forms of letters in various European languages. The invitation is marked " very private and confidential " and conveys with extreme caution and mystery the suggestion that for a sufficient consideration the secret hiding place of a very valuable treasure will be confided to the person addressed. Colour is given to the proposal by some plausible but not always probable story on which it is based.

In one case the writer pretended to be a Spanish officer who had received from the hands of Napoleon III himself, when flying to England in September, 1870, a casket of jewels which he was charged to convey to the Countess of Montijo, mother of the Empress Eugenie, in Madrid. The messenger had however become involved in a Carlist or revolutionary movement and was now in prison, but he had succeeded before arrest in burying the jewels in a remote spot so cleverly concealed that he alone possessed the secret. The liberal offer was made to the person addressed of a fourth share of the total value provided he would transmit to the prisoner correspondent through a sure hand, indicated, the sum of three hundred pounds in cash by means of which he could secure release and proceed to unearth the treasure.

Another story is as follows:

One day the regular mail boat brought to Ceuta an Italian ecclesiastic, a high dignitary of the Church, of grave and venerable appearance, who proceeded at once to make a formal call upon the commandant or general commanding for the time being. He was in search of certain information and he more particularly desired to be directed to an address he sought, that of a small house in a retired spot in one of the small little-frequented streets in the hilly town. He carried with him a heavy and rather bulky handbag which when he started from the general's he begged he might leave in his charge on the plea that its contents were valuable.

After the lapse of two or three hours the Monsignor returned with terrified aspect and evidently in the greatest distress of mind. He entreated that a priest might be summoned to whom he might confess, and his wish was forthwith gratified. The moment he had unbosomed himself to his ghostly adviser, he seized his handbag and ran down to the port just in time to catch the return mail boat to Algeciras. The priest who had heard his confession was to be released from the secret confided to him and reveal it to the authorities as soon as the safe arrival of the mail boat at the mainland was signalled across to Ceuta. Then the whole story came out.

Monsignor X was one of the most trusted and confidential chaplains of his Holiness the Pope and he had gone to Ceuta in the interests of an ex-Carlist general who had the misfortune to be detained there as a political prisoner. A sum of money was needed to compass his escape from the presidio and help him to reach in safety the burying place of a vast treasure, to disinter it and apply it to the furtherance of the civil war in progress. This general seems to have satisfied the papal dignitaries of his identity and good faith; his communication was endorsed with plans and statements pointing to the whereabouts of the hidden treasure, and the method by which the money he needed for his enterprise was to be used, was minutely described. He said he was too closely watched to allow any messenger to reach him direct, but he had friends in Ceuta, two titled ladies, near relatives who had been permitted to live in the prison town and to visit him from time to time and who would pass the money to him when it was brought to Ceuta.

Monsignor X landed as we have seen and learned where he was to go, but with commendable caution he hesitated to take his money with him. He would hand it over when he had made the personal acquaintance of the general's aristocratic friends. They did not prove very desirable acquaintances. He found the house he was to visit, was admitted without question, but then the door was shut behind him and he was murderously assailed by half a dozen convicts, knife in hand. He was ordered to give up the money he had brought, and when on searching him it was found missing, he was rifled of everything he carried in his pockets, both his watch and a considerable sum in cash. His life was spared because it was certain that his prolonged absence would lead to a hue and cry, but he was obliged to swear that he would not attempt to leave the house for one clear hour so that the robbers might make good their escape. Moreover he was warned if he gave the alarm he would certainly be assassinated. Hence his desire to pass beyond the Straits of Gibraltar before the outrage became known. When the house was visited it was found empty and unfurnished with not a sign of life on the premises. The most interesting feature in the story is that the swindlers should fly at such high game, but it is founded on undoubted fact. The Carlist insurrection was often used to father the attempt to defraud.

In another case a letter conveyed to the proprietor of a vineyard at Maestrazgo the alluring news that a large sum in gold was hidden on his ground, the accumulated contributions of Carlist supporters in the neighbourhood. The exact position would be revealed and a plan forwarded in exchange for a sum of four thousand dollars in hard cash, which was to be forwarded to Ceuta according to certain precise instructions. The money was sent but no reply came. Days and weeks passed and at last, weary of waiting and a little unhappy, the easily duped victim made up his mind to cross to Ceuta in person and bring his disappointing correspondent to book. The wine grower unhappily landed in the presidio on the day they were baiting a bull in the streets, a game constantly played and with more danger to the passers-by than the players. The bull goaded into a state of fury attacked the new comer and tossed him so that he fell to the ground with both legs broken. The poor man got no plan and no news of his dollars. All he gained was two months in bed lying between life and death.

The writer Relosillas, who filled the place of an inspector or surveyor of works at Ceuta, has given some of his personal experiences in that convict prison.[1] He describes how on one occasion he was present at a free fight among the convicts in the barracks which had been originally a Franciscan convent. He was in his own office at a late hour, hard by, when he heard a terrible uproar in the great dormitory and ran over to exercise his authority and prevent bloodshed. Knives were out and being freely used by combatants ranged on two sides, one lot backing up a friend who had been robbed of a photograph of his sister, the other lot defending the thief, who had stolen the portrait for use in a buried treasure swindle. He had created her a marchioness and intended to forward it as a bait to show his in-

[1] *Catorce Mese en Ceuta,* Malaga, 1886.

timacy with the aristocracy and prepare the way for the fraud. The case may be quoted to show how minutely the practitioners in the *entierro* studied their ground and acquired the means of operating. In all Spanish prisons and notably in Ceuta, cunning convicts are to be found, men of ability and experience, who have travelled far and wide, who are conversant with many languages and well acquainted with prominent people in other countries and the leading facts and particulars of their lives.

A few additional stories of swindles akin to the *entierro* are of much interest.

A French landowner by name Armand Carron, a resident of a small town in the Department of Finistère, received, some time ago, a letter from Ceuta, signed Santiago (or James) Carron. The writer explained that he was a native of Finistère where the Frenchman resided; that he was a namesake and a member of the landowner's family, son of a first cousin of his who had left France many years before and settled in Spain with wife and three sons, of whom he, Santiago Carron, now alone survived. This Santiago, the letter went on, had been placed by his father in the military college at Segovia, had served through all the subaltern grades as an artillery officer, had risen to the rank of brigadier and in that capacity had been sent out in command of the district of the Cinco Villas in Cuba, where he had married the daughter of Don Diego Calderon, a wealthy Havana merchant, and the

owner of vast sugar plantations. His wife had
brought him a dowry of four million reales (£40,-
000) and had died leaving him a daughter called
after her mother, Juanita, now about 17 years old.
This girl, the only object of her father's love and
care, had been by him sent to Europe and placed for
her education at the convent of the Sacre Cœur at
Chamartin near Madrid.

His career in the army had been for many years
very fortunate and his wedded life in Cuba exceedingly happy. He had been laden with honours by
a grateful Government and received many proofs of
his country's trust, but lately the officer in charge
of the chest of the military district at Cinco Villas
had absconded and run away to New York with
a sum of two million reales. As he, the brigadier,
was answerable for his subaltern's conduct and was
not willing to sacrifice one half of his wife's — now
his daughter's — fortune to pay for the defaulter,
he had been summoned to Spain and then relegated,
or sent as a prisoner on parole to the fortress at
Ceuta to take his trial before a court martial, which
owing to the dilatoriness of all things in Spain
might sit till doomsday.

After thus giving an account of himself and his
belongings the brigadier proceeded to explain the
reasons which induced him to address himself to his
unknown French relative. Having suffered much
from long exposure to the heat of a tropical climate
he felt old before his time, and his hereditary enemy,

the gout, had by several sharp twinges made him
aware of the precariousness of his tenure of life.
He had only that one daughter in the world, the
sole heiress of a considerable patrimony who might
at any moment be deprived of her natural protector
and for whose final education and introduction into
society it was his duty to provide. The girl had
great natural gifts, had inherited her mother's Cre-
ole beauty, and the accounts of her proficiency, given
by the nuns at Chamartin were most flattering to
his paternal pride. He was anxious to appoint a
guardian to his daughter and he could think of no
one fitter in every respect for that charge than his
only relative, M. Armand Carron.

He (the brigadier) had lately been diligently
looking over his father's papers; had found among
them very numerous and interesting family docu-
ments — ample evidence that a hearty and loving
correspondence had for many years been kept up
between his father, Vincent Carron, and the father
of M. Armand Carron, also called Armand, and he
followed up the narrative with frequent allusions to
several incidents occurring in the early youth of the
two cousins, with descriptions of localities, common
acquaintances and the usual joys and sorrows alter-
nating in their domestic circles. Altogether it was
a well contrived, plausible story verging so closely
upon probability as to avoid shipwreck upon the
rock of truth.

M. Armand Carron of Finistère did not think

it right or expedient to cast doubt on the genuineness
of the communication. He answered the brigadier's
appeal by calling him " My dear cousin," saying he
had a perfect recollection of his father's frequent
allusions to Vincent Carron, the cousin who had
grown up with him in their own home and only left
their native town on arriving at man's estate. After
heartily congratulating the brigadier on his conspicuous career which reflected so much lustre on their
own name, and condoling with him about the mo-
mentary cloud that had now — undeservedly he felt
sure — settled upon it, he assured his newly found
relative of his sympathy and of his readiness to look
upon the brigadier's daughter as his own child, to
receive her into the bosom of his family and take
that care of her which so precious a jewel as she was
described to be, must fully deserve.

So the matter was settled. The correspondence
between the two newly found relatives continued for
six or seven months and became very affectionate
and confidential. The brigadier sent the Frenchman
his photograph and that of his daughter, both taken
in Havana and bearing the name and trade mark
of the artist. The one represented a middle-aged
officer of high rank in full uniform and with the
Grand Cross of San Hermengeldo on his breast, a
fine manly countenance with long grey silky mous-
tache; the other exhibiting the arch, pretty countenance of a brunette in her teens, with smooth bands
of raven hair on either side of her low forehead and

the shade of a moonlit night in her dark eyes; a bright blooming creature with dimples and pouting lips and a look of humour and frolic and sense in every feature. Together with the photographs came a letter of Juanita Carron to the brigadier, her father, from the convent, and bearing the Chamartin postmark, in which the girl congratulated her father on his discovery of his Finistère relative, expressed a firm confidence that her loving father would long be spared to her and concluded that she would for her part, in the worst event, willingly acknowledge her relative as a second father and acquiesce in every arrangement that might be made for her welfare.

Seven months passed and the post one morning brought M. Armand Carron a letter with the Ceuta postmark, but no longer in his cousin's handwriting. The writer who signed himself Don Francisco Muñoz, parish priest of San Pedro in Ceuta, announced the death of Brigadier Santiago Carron, which had occurred seven days before the date of the letter. He stated that the brigadier, brought to the last extremity by a sudden attack of gout, had been attended, by him, Don Francisco, as priest in his last hours, and been instructed to wind up all his earthly affairs both in Ceuta and in Madrid. He was further empowered to remove the Señorita Juanita, the brigadier's daughter, from the Chamartin convent and take charge of her during her journey to Finistère where she should be delivered into

the hands of her appointed guardian. The priest's
letter enclosed the printed obituary handbill an-
nouncing the brigadier's decease, according to Spanish custom, the last will and testament of the deceased appointing M. Armand Carron sole executor,
guardian and trustee of his only daughter Juanita,
and entrusting to him the management of her fortune of one million francs, (£40,000), mentioning
the banks in Paris and Amsterdam in which that
sum lay in good state securities. The whole document was duly drawn up by a notary, with witnesses'
signatures, seals, etc., and even with certificates of
the brigadier's burial, the signatures and stamps of
the civil and military authorities at Ceuta and those
of the governor in command of the place.

At the close of this minute statement the priest
expressed his readiness to comply with the brigadier's instructions by travelling to Madrid, receiving the young Juanita from the hands of the Sacre
Cœur nuns and continuing with her the journey to
Finistère, immediately upon hearing from M. Armand Carron that he was prepared to receive his
lovely ward. M. Armand Carron answered by
return of post that his house and arms were open
to welcome his relative's orphan child. Where there
came after some time another letter from Don
Francisco Muñoz explaining that the brigadier, although the most methodical and careful of men, had
left some trifling debts at Ceuta and there were the
doctors' and undertakers' bills to be settled: also

the travelling expenses for himself and the young
lady which he, the priest, was not able to defray.
Besides all this the papers, deeds, books and other
portable property left by the brigadier, some of it
very valuable, but also bulky — among which were
the certificates of the state securities deposited in the
French and Dutch banks — which at the express
desire of the deceased would have at once to be conveyed to Finistère. He, the priest, would have to
be responsible for all this, so that, what with the
boarding money and fees due to the nuns, and the
clothes, linen and other necessaries the young lady
might require to fit herself for appearance in the
world, an expense would have to be incurred of
which it was difficult to calculate the exact amount.
The conclusion was that he could not undertake the
journey unless M. Armand Carron supplied him
with a round sum of money, say four thousand
francs, which he could forward in French bank notes
and in a registered letter addressed not to him but
to a Doña Dolores Mazaredo, a pious woman, whom
her reduced fortunes had compelled to take service
as a washerwoman of the Ceuta state prison.

The reason alleged by the priest for receiving the
money in this roundabout way was that as the brigadier had died in debt to the state and the government
might suspect that property belonging to the deceased had come into his, the priest's charge and
be subject to the law of embargo on the brigadier's effects, it was desirable that every precaution

should be taken to disarm suspicion and prevent injury.

The fraud was entirely successful and in due course the letter from Finistère enclosing bank notes for four thousand francs was delivered to the washerwoman and from her passed into the hands of the sharpers whose deep laid plan and transcendent inventive powers were thus crowned with full success. M. Armand Carron heard no more of his orphaned relative.

The most astonishing feature in the " Spanish Swindle," as it is commonly and almost universally known, is the extent to which it is practised and in countries far remote from those in which the trick originates. In one case a resident in the Argentine Republic received a letter from Madrid which he communicated to the press stating that he could not conceive how his name and address had become known. But it was clear that the Argentine and many other directories were possessed by the swindler, for similar letters all conveying the usual rosy stories of hidden treasure had come into the country wholesale. The fraudulent agent had long discovered that the credulity and cupidity on which he trades are universal weaknesses and that he is likely to find victims in every civilised part of the world. At another time Germany was inundated with typewritten letters from the Spanish prisoner, and the correspondent cleverly accounted for his use of the machine by stating that he was employed as a convict clerk in the office of the governor of the prison.

An attempt of the same kind was tried on a Swiss gentleman of Geneva, but it failed signally. The swindler in Barcelona thought he had beguiled his correspondent into purchasing certain papers at the price of twelve thousand francs by which a treasure was to be found, and sent a young woman to Geneva to receive the cash. But the Swiss police, having been informed of the transaction, were on the alert, and when she kept her appointment with the proposed dupe she was taken into custody. An individual staying at the same hotel and said to have been in communication with her was also arrested. The emissary denied all complicity in the intended fraud protesting that she had been commissioned by a stranger she met in Barcelona to convey a letter to Geneva and bring back another in return.

The ubiquity of the swindle is proved by the adventures of a certain M. Elked, a restaurateur of Buda-Pest, who was lured into making a journey to Madrid, carrying with him a sum of ten thousand francs in cash. The money was to be used in securing possession of a fortune of three hundred thousand francs, part of which was lying in a trunk deposited in the cloak room of a French railway station and part in the strong room of a Berlin bank. Elked was to get the half in return for his advance. On arrival in Madrid he met the representative of his correspondent and was shown bogus receipts from the railway and bank. To remove all possible doubt it was suggested that telegrams should be sent to the railway station and to the bank and in due course what purported to be replies were brought to Elked by a pretended telegraph messenger. The sham telegrams finally convinced him of the genuineness of the business and he arranged to meet the swindler in a certain café to hand over the ten thousand francs.

All this time an eye was kept upon Elked by a brother Hungarian named Isray, a commercial traveller, who had come to Madrid by the same train and who on hearing the purpose of the restaurateur's visit had vainly tried to persuade him that the affair was a fraud. Isray followed his infatuated compatriot to the café in a very low quarter of Madrid and arrived just in time to see three men attempting to hustle Elked into a carriage. He had apparently hesitated to hand over the money at the last moment and the ruffians were attempting to get him away to a spot where he could be conveniently searched and robbed. Isray drew his revolver and fired two or three shots at Elked's assailants, but did not succeed in hitting any one. He contrived however to injure the horse and the struggle ended in the three bandits running away, leaving Elked still in possession of his money. No passers-by offered the Hungarians any assistance during the fight, nor did any police appear on the scene. When Elked subsequently complained to the police authorities they simply laughed at him for displaying so much credulity. The victims of the " Spanish Swindle " are certainly not entitled to much sympathy. Although arrests are occasionally made, the Spanish police have never been able to cope very successfully with the ancient and ever flourishing fraud.

Some of the Spanish prisoner's lies are the crudest and most transparent attempts at fraud, but a few are really very fine works of art. An English country gentleman once received the following letter:

" DEAR SIR AND RELATIVE: Not having the honour to know you but for the reference which my dead wife, Mary — your relative — gave me, who in detailing the various individuals of our family warmly praised the honest and good qualities which distinguished you, I now address myself to you for the first time and perhaps for the last one considering the grave state of my health, explaining my sad position and requesting your protection for my only daughter, a child of fourteen years old whom I keep as a pensioner in a college — "

This is the prelude to a really clever and picturesque story of the writer's adventures in Cuba, where, after having been secretary and treasurer to Martinez Campos, he had subsequently been driven by General Weyler to join the insurgents, and was eventually forced to flee the country taking with him his fortune of thirty-seven thousand pounds. Subse-

quently being summoned to Spain by the illness of
his " only daughter child " he deposited the money
in a London bank under the form of " security document."   After this we are introduced to the old
mechanism of this venerable swindle.   The deposited note was concealed in a secret drawer of the
prisoner's portmanteau.   The prisoner had been arrested on his arrival in Spain, but a trusty friend
at large was willing to assist him in recovering the
money for the benefit of his child, if only the dear
relative in England " would advance the necessary
funds for expenses."   It is possible to imagine that
anyone who had never heard of these ingenious
frauds might be taken in by such a plausible narrative, but it is difficult to understand such ignorance.
A letter was received from the Castle of Montjuich
in Barcelona by a man in Dublin, who showed it to
several friends in the city explaining the process.
It was new to them all, and arrests of persons who
had all but succeeded in completing this well-worn
confidence trick are constantly made in London.
The boldness of these attempts may be seen in the
case of the swindlers who despatched three letters
identically the same, to three persons who were near
neighbours, residing at North Berwick near Edin-
burgh.   The letter dated from Madrid and said : —

" Sir, Detained here as a bankrupt, I ask if you
would help me to withdraw the sum of fr. 925,000
(£37,000) at present lodged in a secure place in

France. It would be necessary for you to visit Madrid and obtain possession of my baggage by paying a lien on it. In one valise concealed in a secret niche is the document which must be produced as a warrant for the delivery of the above mentioned sum. I propose to hand you over a third of the whole in return for your outlay and trouble."

The rest of the letter simply contained instructions as to telegraphing an answer to Madrid. The whole was a very stupid and clumsy attempt to deceive, lacking all the emotional appeals, the motherless child, the persecuted political adherent of a failing cause. Worse yet it openly invited co-operation with a bankrupt seeking to defraud his creditors. Nor is there any effort to explain the selection of these three particular persons in the same small town as parties to the fraud, and the only conclusion is that dupes had been found even under such circumstances who were afterward reluctant to reveal their own foolishness.

A more elaborate fraud was perpetrated soon after the fall of Cartagena; the story ran as follows: Two of the well known leaders of the harebrained republican movement that led to that catastrophe, — General Contreras and Señor Galdez, — both deputies of the Constituent Cortes, came as fugitives to England and lodged in the Bank of England a sum amounting to several millions of reales in state securities, obtaining for them of course the

regular certificates and receipt from the bank.
These two Spanish gentlemen afterwards lived for
some time on the continent. General Contreras
took up his quarters as a political exile in France
and Señor Galdez ventured under a disguise into
Spain, where he had the misfortune to be recognised,
arrested and shut up in the Saladero. The certificates had been left in England in trusty hands, in a
trunk belonging to Señor Galdez, who from his
prison sent directions that the box should be sent by
rail to Madrid addressed to a person enjoying his
full confidence. This person however had some
claim upon Señor Galdez for an old debt of six
thousand francs or about two hundred and forty
pounds and insisted upon payment of this sum before
he would either part with the trunk or allow it to
be opened and the precious certificates to be taken
from it.

The matter required delicate handling, for Señor
Galdez was a prisoner, General Contreras an exile,
both beyond reach, and about the money they had
placed in the bank there might lie some mystery into
which it was not desirable that enquiry should be
made. An easy way of getting at the contents of
the trunk could be found if any one would think it
worth while to supply two hundred and forty
pounds, settle the claims of Señor Galdez's creditor,
and laying hold of the certificates, convey them to
England and withdraw the securities from the bank.
A man whose name was given and whose address

was in the Calle de la Abada or Rhinoceros Street, Madrid, would undertake to carry through the negotiations if any one would call upon him with the needful two hundred and forty pounds and allow him half an hour to rescue the trunk and deliver the certificates. The worthy Yorkshire squire to whom intimation had been conveyed of the coup there was to be made, looked upon the story as extremely probable. He fancied it was corroborated by a good deal of circumstantial evidence and thought he might venture on the speculation. A professional adviser whom he consulted undertook to do the job for him and carry the two hundred and forty pounds to the Calle de la Abada, taking a revolver with him, as a precaution, and intending to deliver the money in Bank of England notes, the numbers of which should be stopped the moment he found out that any trick was being played on his good faith.

Further enquiries were made, however, before any decided steps were taken, and it was ascertained beyond doubt that Señor Galdez was no longer a prisoner, that General Contreras had come back from banishment, that the house in the Calle de la Abada was a notorious haunt of malefactors and den of thieves, and the whole scheme was another instance of the criminal ingenuity of the Spanish swindler.

CHAPTER VIII

LIFE IN CEUTA

Dangerous weapons manufactured within the prison walls —
Frequent quarrels — Murderous assaults on warders of constant occurrence — Disorders and lack of discipline owing
to the employment of prisoners as warders — The *"cabos
de vara"* — These posts sold to the highest bidder — Salillas' description of these convict warders — Worst criminals often promoted to exercise authority over their fellows
— Terrible evils arising from such a state of affairs — Description of Ceuta — Life at Ceuta no deterrent to crime by
reason of the pleasant conditions under which the convicts
lived — Popularity of the theatre in Spanish prisons — Escapes from Ceuta — The case of El Nino de Brenes — The
different characteristics of the Andalusians and Aragonese
— Foreigners from Spanish colonies imprisoned at Ceuta —
Chinamen and negroes — Dolores, the negro convict — His
assassination by two fellow convicts — Political prisoners
— Carlists — Different types of murderers.

LIFE is held cheap in Ceuta and indeed in all
Spanish presidios and gaols. The saying " a word
and a blow," may be expanded into " a word and a
knife thrust." The possession of a lethal weapon
is common to all prisoners and prevails despite pro-
hibiting regulations. Fatal affrays are of constant
occurrence. At Valladolid five men were wounded

in a fight over cards, which were openly permitted. An official enquiry followed, with the result that on a search instituted through the prison, numbers of large knives were discovered and many smaller daggers.

It is pretended by the authorities that the introduction of such weapons as well as of spirits and packs of cards cannot be prevented. The gate keepers however exercise no vigilance or are readily bribed to shut their eyes. The ruinous condition of many gaols with their numerous cracks and openings and holes in the walls is partially responsible. As a natural consequence blood flowed freely when rage and unbridled passion were so easily inflamed and the means of seeking murderous satisfaction were always ready to hand. Quarrels grew at once into fierce fights which could not be prevented and must be fought out then and there even to the death. Chains and stone walls and iron bars were ineffective in imposing order. There could be no semblance of discipline where the two essentials were absolutely wanting, supervision and honest service in the keepers.

Knives were often provided by the ingenious adaptation of all kinds of material within the walls, such as one-half of a pair of scissors firmly fixed in a handle bound round with cloth; or a piece of tin doubled to form a blade and stiffened by two pieces of wood to keep the point sharp; or the handle of a wooden spoon sharpened and as formidable as

an inflexible fish bone.[1]   Other arms carried and
used on occasion for premeditated or unexpected
attack or in set, formal encounters were a razor, a
file, a carpenter's adze, a hammer, a cobbler's awl.

Some surprising figures have been collected by
Salillas to show how frequent was the appeal to violence and how fatal the consequences of the bloodthirsty strife so constantly breaking out among the
more reckless members of this hot-tempered Latin
race.   They had often their origin in drunken quarrels, for *aguardiente,* the Spanish equivalent to whis-
key or gin, was always plentiful, introduced almost
openly by the warders.   Ancient feuds were revived
when the opportunity of settling them was offered
by the chance meeting in the gaol.   Occasionally a
homicidal lunatic ran loose about the yards and
struck blindly at any inoffensive person he met when
the furious fit was on him.   Salillas tells us that in
one year sixteen murderous assaults were committed
upon warders,[2] and twenty-four free fights occurred
among the prisoners, eleven of whom were killed
outright and forty-two seriously wounded.   One
truculent ruffian fell upon an aged wardsman (a
convict also), struck him with a shoemaker's knife

---

[1] I have seen a precisely similar weapon in an English convict prison, the product of an evil-minded prisoner who used
it in an assault upon his officer.

[2] An official report dated 1888 gives a total of 221 prisoners
in the whole of the establishments admitted into hospital suffering from wounds, fractures and contusions received in the
gaols.

and then, brandishing his weapon, defied interference or the rescue of his victim whom he " finished " with repeated blows. A Valencian newspaper describes an encounter between two inmates of the Torres Serranos prison in that city. " Without warning or suggesting the cause of difference the two silently hurried to a large empty room, rushed at each other with their knives, and the only sounds heard were those of blows struck and warded off and of shuffling feet as they circled round each other. Warders headed by the governor (alcaide) strove to separate the combatants and succeeded at last in doing so but at peril of their lives. Both the antagonists were wounded, one had his cheek laid open and the other's face was horribly gashed. At Saragossa an old man who complained that one of his blankets had been stolen was fiercely attacked in the shoemaker's shop by the thief, who had been cutting out sole leather with a heavy iron tool. Deadly wounds were inflicted on the victim, but the infuriated aggressor stood over him, keeping those who would have interposed at bay until it was clearly evident that death had supervened.

The primary cause of the chronic discreditable, disgraceful disorder that reigned in the Spanish prisons was the prevailing custom of employing prisoners in the service and discipline of the prisons. This practice is now universally condemned as reprehensible and it has been abolished in most civilised countries and even in Spain. The excuse offered

which long passed current in Spain was the expense
entailed by employing a proper staff of officers, a
necessity in every well ordered prison administration.   But till quite a recent date the control and
supervision of prisoners in Spanish gaols was practically their own affair.   There were the usual superior officials, assisted by a few free overseers (*capa-
taces*) but the bulk of the work was entrusted to
the *cabos de vara.*

The vicious system was the more objectionable
from the uncertainty which prevailed in its working.
If the *cabo de vara* had been carefully selected from
the best and most exemplary prisoners some of the
worst evils might have been avoided.   But it was
all a matter of chance.   Not only was there no selection of the best but there was no rejection or elimi-
nation of the worst candidates.   In some conspicuous cases the office of *cabo de vara* was suffered to
fall into the hands of men altogether unfit to hold
it.   Two in particular may be quoted, those of
Pelufo and Carrillo, who having first committed
atrocious crimes, escaped punishment and were actually promoted.   One, Pelufo, was a convict in the
presidio of Cartagena who murdered a *cabo* and cut
his way out of the St. Augustin prison, knife in
hand; the other, Carrillo, slew a comrade in a duel
in the presidio of San Miguel de los Reyes (Valencia) and both were subsequently appointed *cabos,*
" a reward," as a witty official said, " which they had
earned by their services to penitentiary methods."

With such examples and under such authorities serious crimes were naturally numerous. A few may be mentioned. A *cabo* named Casalta killed a fellow *cabo* in St. Augustin prison of Valencia with five cruel thrusts and afterwards stabbed an officer to the heart. When the military guard came up he seriously injured one of the soldiers and wounded two convicts, one in the head, the other in the back. Casalta was however condemned to a fresh sentence of twelve years. One Ferreiro Volta cut a comrade's throat for having given evidence against the man, Pelufo, already mentioned. Many more cases of the same heinous character where the homicidal instinct had full play may be picked out of the published lists. In one prison thirteen already guilty of murder or attempted murder repeated their crimes as prisoners; in another nine convicted of maliciously wounding, pursued the practice or were guilty of awful threats to murder in the gaols. The cases might be multiplied almost indefinitely but it will suffice to indicate the terrible conditions constantly prevailing. No doubt murderous attacks were often stimulated by the tyranny of the prisoner *cabos,* against whom their fellows, goaded to desperation, rose and wreaked vengeance.

The discipline exercised by these prisoner warders was naturally not worth much. It was their duty to correct and restrain their comrades, to assist in their pursuit when they escaped after having originally most probably facilitated the evasion, to side with the authority in cases of serious insubordination and disturbance. But they were weak vessels yielding readily to temptation, accepting bribes hungrily, swallowing drink greedily when offered, quickly cowed by the threats of prison bullies and surrendering at discretion when opposed. But even although there were good and trusty men to be found at times among them, no real reliance could be placed in them. They generally represented fifty per cent. of the staff and the necessity for the substitution of the non-convicted, properly paid, fairly honourable warders has been very wisely decided upon. The chief danger lay in their close and intimate association with the rest, day and night constantly alone when no official supervision was possible. Their value depended entirely upon their personal qualifications. If they were weak-kneed and invertebrate, they could apply no check upon the ill-conditioned, could neither intimidate nor repress: if on the other hand they were of masterful character with arrogant, overbearing tempers, they might do immense mischief by tyrannising over their charges and leading them astray. Men of this class often claimed an equality with the recognised officials, treated them with off-hand familiarity, spoke without saluting or removing their caps, while insolently puffing the smoke of a half-consumed cigarette in faces of the officers. Salillas sums up the type as " semi-functionary, semi-convict and all hangman."

The external aspect of Ceuta is not unpleasing.
It is built on seven hills, the highest of which is
topped by the fortress, and in the word "septem"
we may trace the name Ceuta. It still possesses a
few Moorish remains, for it was once an important
Moorish city. Some of the streets show a tesselated
pavement of red, white and green tiles, and house
fronts are to be seen in white, black and serpentine
marble with decorated scroll work running in a pat-
tern below the gutter. It has some claims to be
picturesque and possesses certain artistic architectural features. An imposing barrack, that called
Del Valle, built by prison labour, is considered one
of the finest Spanish military edifices. It has also
a cathedral dedicated to Our Lady of Africa, engi-
neering and artillery yards, a military hospital, another church, public offices, and above all a palace
of the governor and general commanding. The
latter in particular, with its extensive grounds, handsome façade, and suites of fine rooms, the whole
well mounted and served by a large staff of convict
attendants, is the envy of all other government officials. One wide street traverses the city from west
to east crossed by a network of smaller ways, all
airy and well ventilated by sea breezes and constantly illuminated by a brilliant sun. From time
to time convicts in their distinctive dress pass along,
but scarcely cast a shadow upon the scene, showing
few signs of their thraldom and passing along with
light-hearted freedom, smoking excellent tobacco or

singing a gay song. No beggars offend the eye, for
to solicit public charity is strictly forbidden. Generally a contented well-to-do air is worn by the
crowd, and even the convicts are decently dressed.
Other inhabitants, Moors from the mainland, and
Jews long established in commerce seem prosperous
and evidently possess ample means gained by their
industry and thrift.

The presidio or prison proper of Ceuta covers a
large part of the peninsula or promontory and em-
braces four distinct districts; the first is situated in
the new or modern town; the second lies just outside it; the third is within the old town and the
fourth is beyond the outer line of walls. The first
part is connected with the third by a drawbridge
called *boquete de la sardina* or the " sardine's entrance "; the second with the third by a portcullis;
the third with the fourth and last by the outer gate
of the city.

In the first are the artisans' quarters, situated in
the cloisters of an ancient monastery, that of San
Francisco, and but for the patching and whitewash-
ing would look quite ruinous. It is neither secure
nor of sufficient size. The night guards are posted
in the old mortuary house, the bars to many windows are of wood. The building contains offices,
schoolhouse, store for clothing and the workshops,
these being in a sort of patio or courtyard, or in
hollow spaces in the cloisters, and are simply dens
and rookeries, in part exactly over the old burial

ground. The handicrafts pursued when I visited it were various: men were making shoes; fourteen tailors were at work; a blacksmith with a life sentence constantly hammered out the red hot iron; a tinsmith produced many useful articles; a turner at his lathe worked admirably in the old meat bones and fashioned handles for walking sticks and umbrellas. This turner earned much money and was comfortably lodged. Convicts at Ceuta are not deprived of their profits and spend their money buying better food, superior clothing and *aguardiente* and using it to bribe their overseers, or they cleverly conceal it, adding constantly to their store. Industry is a chief source of wealth, but many political prisoners bring large sums in with them, or it is smuggled in to them, and a successful hit with the " buried treasure fraud " will supply plenty of cash.

Other industries followed are carpentering and the construction of trunks and boxes which sell well. A number of looms are engaged in weaving canvas for the manufacture of sails for the local shipping, rough material for sacking and clothing of the convicts, all in large quantities and to a really valuable extent. These workshops are filled by the prisoners in the first stage of their detention. The water-carriers and clerks in the government office are in the second period, and on reaching the third the convicts obtain the privilege of going at large to accept employment in the town " from gun to gun."

The prison hospital is situated in this first district,

an ancient edifice erected with part of the funds
subscribed in times past to purchase freedom for
Christian captives enslaved by the Barbary Moors.
The building is of good size, well ventilated, and en-
joys good hygienic conditions. But the defects and
shortcomings in Spanish administration extend even
to Ceuta and the prison hospital, which a local authority says "is detestably organised and mounted
miserably." The roof is so slight that it affords
no proper protection in summer and the intense heat
of the blazing sun striking through is very injuri-
ous to the patients. The medical resources are
small and inferior; the beds few and unclean; the
whole of the interior arrangements, furniture fit-
tings and appliances, insufficient and worn out.
There is no mortuary and to add a small detail in
proof of the imperfections, autopsies were performed in a small den, part of the hospital proper,
without disinfectants and the essential appliances for
carrying out post mortems. Patients seldom made
a long stay in the hospital, for they were rarely admitted until they had reached the last stages of an
illness and came in as a rule only to die.

The second district contains the principal quarters
for convicts. One is in the chief barrack called
cuartel principal and another in the fortress *el
Hacho*.[1] Some further evidence of their evil condition may be extracted from an account given by
Salillas. "It is impossible to conceive," he writes,

[1] See ante, pp. 159 sqq.

" a more unsuitable, unsavoury place for a prison.
The rooms and dormitories occupied by the convicts
are dark and gloomy, always damp, full of pestilen-
tial odours and dirty beyond description.   The floors
are of beaten earth, ever secure hiding places for all
forbidden articles, weapons, tools for compassing
escape, jars of drink, the fiery and poisonous *aguardiente*. It seems to me extraordinary," he goes on
to say, " that life under such conditions is possible.
A thousand and odd men who seldom if ever wash,
who never change their clothes, are crowded together promiscuously in small, unclean, ill-ventilated,
noisome dens and must surely engender and propa-
gate loathsome epidemic disease."   The fetid air is
foul with the noisome exhalations of many generations of pestiferous people. It is one sink of concentrated malaria — a reeking hot bed of infection.
The services of supply are carried out with abominable carelessness : the kitchen is an abode of nasti-
ness : the cooking is performed by repulsive looking
convicts in greasy rags who plunge their dirty arms
deep into the seething mess of soup which they bail
out into buckets, a malodorous compound of the
colour and consistency of the mortar used in building a wall.

Close by is another quarter in which convicts are
lodged, *el Hacho*, or the hilly ground or topmost
point of Ceuta on which is placed the citadel which
crowns the fortifications. It takes the overflow from
the principal barrack and is moreover generally oc-

cupied by the worst characters, the most insubordinate and incorrigible members of the prison population. The rooms, as in the barrack below, are dirty, overcrowded and insecure, but a few windows of the upper story open on to the Mediterranean and are not always protected by either wooden or iron bars. *El Hacho* contains within its limits a certain number of solitary cells, well known and much dreaded by the habitual criminals of Spain. They are essentially punishment cells used in the coercion of the incorrigible and are just as dark, damp and wretched as the larger rooms. But the solitary inmate in each cell is generally kept chained to the wall or is as it is styled *amarrado en blanca,* nearly naked and heavily ironed. The treatment is exemplary in its cruelty, but does not necessarily cure the subject. There was one irreclaimable upon whom several years of the *calabozo* had had no effect. He had been sentenced to be thus chained up as the penalty for murderously wounding an overseer in *el Hacho*, but he did not mend his manners. On one occasion on the arrival of a new governor all under punishment were pardoned. This convict when sent out forthwith furiously attacked the first warder he met and was again condemned to be locked up as a ceaseless danger to the presidio. He is remembered as little more than a youth, but with a diabolical countenance and indomitable air.

The district of the *Barcas* does not contain a barrack properly speaking, but there is a space cut in the thickness of the line wall entering a patio or courtyard which gives upon seven rooms, some high, some low; of these three and part of the yard were filled with munitions of war, and a battery of artillery was placed over the dormitories on their upper floor. Many of the convicts are employed as boatmen and watchmen in the port, others have charge of the walls and carry water up to the guardhouses on the higher level. They also attend to the service of the drawbridge between the old and new town. One who was employed as gatekeeper at the drawbridge was well remembered. He was trusted to call on all convicts who passed to produce their permits of free circulation or to enter and leave the fortress. He had a pleasant rubicund face, was one armed, a little deaf, but with very sharp eyes, not easily hoodwinked. He was a confirmed gossip who picked up all the news which he retailed to all who passed in and out. Escapes were of constant occurrence at Ceuta, but few occurred by the drawbridge of the *Barcas*.

Half way up the road from the town to the citadel and the fort of the Seraglio was the Jadu barrack which was occupied by the convicts who were engaged in agricultural work, in making tiles and burning charcoal. Many of these were foreigners and negroes. The bulk of the residents was made up of those who had completed three fourths of their sentences and lived "under conditions," or in a state of conditional or semi-freedom. There was little wrong-doing in Jadu, thefts were rare, fights and quarrels seldom took place. The Seraglio was a fortified barrack of rectangular shape occupied by troops of the garrison and lodging an odd hundred convicts labouring on adjacent farms in private hands.

It will be observed that the convicts established in these last-named quarters beyond the walls do not appear to exhibit all the unpleasant features attributed to them by some writers in recording their experiences of Ceuta.[1] No doubt the truth lies somewhere between the two extremes but it is certain that the chief penal colony of Spain shares to a marked extent the drawbacks inseparable from all forms of penal colonisation. We may see, beyond all question, that at Ceuta no beneficial results are achieved by the system. Criminals who undergo the penalty are not improved by it; their reformation, too generally a will-o'-the-wisp under the very best auspices, is not even attempted, much less assured. On the other hand, it is perfectly clear that evil is perpetually in the ascendent, that criminal tendencies are largely encouraged by the facilities given in the education and practice of wrong doing; that the presidio itself is a criminal centre where the seeds of crime are sown and their growth fostered despite the difficulties of distance and inconvenience. The fear of penal exile is no deterrent to crime for the simple reason that life in Ceuta is not particu-

[1] See ante, p. 159.

larly irksome and that the convict finds many com-
pensations there. The obligation to hard labour is
not strictly enforced. Man must work, but not hard
and chiefly for his own advantage, to gain the
means of softening and bettering his lot. He passes
his time very much as he pleases. Though he rises
with the sun, as is the universal custom of his country, he turns out of bed without giving a thought to
personal cleanliness and proceeds to his appointed
labour leisurely, after disposing of his breakfast,
adding perhaps more toothsome articles of food, including a morning drink of *aguardiente* bought
from the hawkers and hucksters awaiting him at the
prison gates. He is dressed in prison uniform, but
it is sufficient and suitably varied with the season.
He is not hampered by fetters, as the ancient practice of chaining convicts together in couplets has
long since ceased. The wearing of irons fell into
disuse years ago at the building of the great barrack
del Valle, when several deplorable accidents occurred and it was found that chains interfered with
the free movement of workmen on scaffolding and
so forth. The idea was that irons should again be
imposed at the conclusion of the building; "but all
who thought so did not know Spanish ways, nor
the despotism of custom when once established." [1]
"To-day (1873)," says the same writer, "there are
not fifty suits of chains in the storehouse and not
more than twenty are worn by special penalty and

[1] Relosillas.

by no means as a general practice." The convict
loafs about the rooms or courtyard or idly handles
the tools of his trade, gossiping freely with his comrades, or taking a hand at *monte* or *chapas* with the
full permission of warders not indisposed to have
a " little on the games "; he finds easy means to
issue into the streets to carry on some delectable
flirtation; there may be a bull baiting afoot, a
novillos in which all may join, or a theatrical performance is being given by a convict company in
one of the penal establishments.

The theatre is a passion with the average Spaniard and the taste extends to those in durance.
Cases constantly occur in which popular plays have
been reproduced in prisons situated in the principal
cities.   Salillas [1] states that almost all the prisons
of Spain had their theatre and he gives the names of
Burgos, Ceuta, Ocana, Valladolid, Saladero (Madrid) and Alcala de Henares.   One writer who visited the prison performance at Seville of a musical
piece, the " Viejas Ricas de Cadiz," said it was given
well and that the vocal talent was considerable in
that and other prisons.   At the presidio of San
Miguel de los Reyes the convicts were heard singing a chorus on Christmas Eve which was perfectly
executed and with great feeling.

In the Valladolid gaol the theatre was regularly
installed by a company of forty convicts who had
contributed substantial sums for the purpose.   It

[1] "Vida Penal en Espana."

had working committees with rules and regulations formally sanctioned by the governor of the province. The theatre with seats for an audience of four hundred, and four private boxes holding twelve persons each, was constructed in a building which afterwards became the blacksmith shops. A refreshment room was provided in which a contractor dispensed sweets and pastry and strong drink; real actresses were engaged from outside at a salary of a dollar for each performance; invitations were issued to the free residents and the convicts paid two reales for admission. Well known, high class plays were produced, comedies, dramas and comic operas.

The whole proceeding was a caricature upon prison discipline and the authorities who permitted it were very properly sharply and severely condemned. They exposed themselves to reproof and worse for flagrant contempt of the most ordinary restrictions in allowing women to pass in constantly, and in permitting the sale of alcoholic liquors. That a place of durance, primarily intended for the restraint and punishment of evil doers should be converted into a show and spectacle was an intolerable misuse of power and a disgraceful travesty of the fitness of things. The positive evil engendered was seen in the wholesale escape of the theatrical company, while the audience patiently waited in front of the curtain which "went up" eventually on a wholly unexpected performance.[1]

[1] See ante, p. 128.

In the matter of escapes Ceuta was famous. **It** was not difficult to get away from that imperfectly guarded stronghold when the convict had means to bribe officers or buy a boat and had the courage to make the voyage across the Straits of Gibraltar. The story of one veteran convict who escaped from Ceuta is interesting because he was driven to take himself off by what he no doubt deemed the ill-judged severity of his injudicious keepers. This was an old brigand known as " *El Niño de Brenes,*" (the lad of Brenes), a name he must have earned some time back for he was a man aged seventy when he "withdrew" (the word is exact) from Ceuta. He was a well-behaved, well-to-do convict of affable address who had gained many staunch friends among the officials and his own comrades. The position he had created for himself was one of practical ease and comfort; he lived in *el Hacho* pursuing various industries, usury among the rest, and gradually grew so rich that he gained possession of a strip of land which he cultivated profitably and kept a fine poultry yard as well as many sheep and goats.

El Niño was a tall well built old man, dark-skinned, with abundant white hair. He was of highly respectable appearance, very stout and sleek, and, being on the best of terms with his masters, he took upon himself to discard the prison uniform and dress himself as an Andalusian peasant with gaiters and red sash and *sombrero calañes* (round

hard hat). Not strangely this presumption dis-
pleased the authorities and he was told that he must
conform to the rules and appear in the proper convict clothing and cease to act as a money lender to
his poorer brethren. He received this intimation
with a smiling protest; he pointed out that he used
his influence in pacifying ill-conditioned convicts, in
staving off disturbances and preventing quarrels.
If his services were not better appreciated and he
was tied down to the strict observance of the ordinary rules he would move further away; his remaining in the presidio was quite a matter of favour
and he had always at his disposal the means to make
his escape, and if he were interfered with he would
take his departure. This impudent reply quite ex-
asperated the authorities, who thereupon resolved to
employ sharp measures. The facts as he had stated
them were more or less true and the blame lay really
with the faulty and inefficient régime in force. But
the authorities would not tamely submit to be defied
and a peremptory order was issued that he should
dispose of his private property by a certain date,
wind up his financial affairs and renounce all idea of
exceptional treatment. El Niño took this as a
threat to which there could be but one reply. He
gathered together his cash and portable property
and quietly disappeared. A hue and cry was raised;
the usual signals flew at the signal staff; all gates
and exits were closely watched; the police were unceasingly active in pursuit, but the fugitive had laid

his plans astutely and was never recaptured. Having the command of ample means he doubtless used them freely to purchase freedom by taking some sure road past the frontier or across the sea.

Allies and auxiliaries were never wanting to the enterprising fugitive willing to pay liberally for assistance. In one case a convict had the courage to allow himself to be shut up in a chest half full of tobacco and to be thus conveyed to Gibraltar, to which it was returned as containing damaged goods. Gibraltar is a free port and the chest was landed without question. Then the consignee opened it without delay and extracted the fugitive convict uninjured. The last part of the story is somewhat incredible and we may wonder why the fugitive did not succumb to the discomforts of his narrow receptacle, want of air, the exhalations of the tobacco and the shakings and bumping of the box as it made its voyage, albeit a short one, from Ceuta to the Rock.

An escape on a large scale was effected from the principal barrack when eighteen convicts descended into the drains, and finding their progress unimpeded threaded them safely and passing under the outer wall reached the outlet to the sea. It happened that the water was high and that there was a great conflict of currents in which that setting inward had most force and the exit was blocked by the stormy waves. Some of the convicts committed themselves to the waters but were washed back with violence against the rocky fortifications and all of them in terror for their lives raised loud cries, calling for help. The sentries gave the alarm, the guards ran down and recaptured all the fugitives but one, a fine swimmer who persisted in his attempt and was swept seaward clear of the rough water till he was able to regain the shore on the far side of the Moorish sentries.

The prison population of Ceuta is made up of a number of motley, polyglot types of the many diverse families that compose the Spanish race and of other distinct nationalities. The Spaniards are generally classified under two principal heads: the Aragonese and the Andalusians. The first named comprises all from the northern provinces who are generally coarse, quarrelsome and brutal, sentenced chiefly for crimes of violence, murders premeditated and committed under aggravated circumstances, the outcome of furious and ungovernable passion. The Andalusian is of more generous character, lively and light-hearted, but of unsettled disposition and much impelled to attempt escapes. He is a chronic grumbler constantly moved to complain, dissatisfied with his rations and clamorous for special privileges. The Aragonese on the other hand suffers long in silence which leads eventually, after long brooding, into mutinous combination. The Andalusian makes his grievances heard by word of mouth, the Aragonese rushes without notice into overt action and organised attack. Another distinct section of the Spanish race is the Galician and the native of the

Asturias, a sober, quiet and well-conducted people at home, who exhibit great ferocity as convicts. Sanguinary encounters are little known in these provinces, but when an Asturian or Galician takes the life of his enemy, he uses artifice and waylays him, decoying him into an ambush and murdering him often with horrible mutilation. A criminal feature, peculiar to the women of these provinces, is their addiction to the use of poison. Other Spanish females will use violence and inflict lethal wounds openly, but the Galician woman administers poison secretly, deliberately choosing her victims among her nearest relatives.

The colonial empire of Spain, now a thing of the past, contributed in its time a substantial contingent of yellow and black convicts, Chinamen from the Philippines and negroes from Cuba. It was a reprehensible practice to associate these foreigners with the European convicts and it produced many evils. The Chinaman was often shamefully ill-treated. He bore it patiently, but at times when goaded beyond endurance, retaliated with bloodthirsty violence. The story of one negro convict, a rather remarkable person, is still remembered at Ceuta. He rejoiced in the somewhat inappropriate feminine name of Dolores, and despite his colour was a singularly handsome man. He had a slight, active figure, a highly intelligent face and a clear, penetrating eye. His mental faculties were of a high order, although he had received only an indifferent education. He had the fondness of his race for fine clothes and although conforming to the prison uniform wore it with a certain distinction, improving and adding to it where possible and having quite a gentlemanly appearance. He had been guilty of a hideous murder in Havana for which he had received a nearly interminable sentence. His behaviour in gaol was orderly and submissive and he always displayed the utmost loyalty to his masters, who in return lightened his lot as far as was possible.

Dolores, as a rule, was of a patient disposition, although he was easily roused into fits of violent temper and could be at times, according to his treatment, either a lion or a lamb. It seemed almost incomprehensible that the mild eyes so calm and peaceable, when he was unmoved, could blaze with sudden fury or that his small delicately shaped hands could fasten murderously on a fellow creature's throat. Tyranny and oppression were intolerable to him and he altogether declined to submit to be domineered over by the chief bully in the prison. His defiance led to an embittered conflict — a duel fought out with knives — in which the black champion conquered after inflicting many deep wounds upon his antagonist. With his victory Dolores gained also the implacable ill-will of his fellows. They put him on his trial, in a corner of the principal barrack and condemned him to death, which would certainly have been inflicted had not the authorities interposed to give him their protection.

He was removed to *el Hacho* and placed in one of
the separate cells used generally for the punishment
of the incorrigible.[1]   This was fatal to him.   Two
water-carriers belonging to the hostile faction entered the cell when Dolores was engaged in writing
with his back to the door, and throwing themselves
upon him gave him two mortal wounds under the
left shoulder.   In this supreme moment Dolores put
forth his tremendous strength, caught his assailants
by their necks and broke them before the warders
could interfere on either side.   Dolores died but he
is still remembered in the prison annals as one of
the most valiant and indomitable convicts who had
ever been detained in the presidio.

Another alien convict to whom Relosillas pays a
high tribute was his own Chinese servant, a convict
known as " Juan de la Cruz, the Asiatic."   He
seems to have been unceasingly loyal and devoted
in his service, an admirable cook, an indefatigable
nurse, a faithful watchman who guarded his effects
and secured his privacy.   Juan had many accom-
plishments; he could weave shade hats of the finest
palm fibre, he was as clever as any seamstress with
his needle; he was a first-class housemaid and laun-
dress; he could make a dollar go further in the
market than the most economical housewife.   He
drove the most astonishing bargains with the hucksters and purveyors of food, fish and game, with
which Ceuta was plentifully supplied.   He had been

[1] See ante, p. 194.

condemned to a long term for a murder committed in Havana at a hotel, of which he was the chief cook. In appearance he was younger than his years, tall, thin, anæmic looking, shortsighted, with jet black hair and oblique eyes. He was a man of great intelligence, a dramatic author in Chinese and was released before his time to accompany the Director General of Prisons to Madrid as his cook. In the end he started a fruit shop in the capital and prospered greatly.

An entirely different class of prisoners came to Ceuta in considerable numbers from time to time, — those exiled for political misdeeds. A whole discipline battalion was composed of military offenders, among them a number of artillerymen condemned for the rising in Barcelona and crowds of Carlists and those concerned in the so-called cantonal risings. One or two politicals were strange characters, such as the old soldier named " el Cojo " (the lame man) of Cariñena, a conceited veteran very proud of his many campaigns in which he had served, and who went everywhere on donkey back, being infirm and crippled. Another was the ex-curé of Berraonda, a Biscayan priest of ferocious aspect, tall, corpulent, dark-skinned, with an abundant snow white bushy beard, which grew to his waist and which was left untouched by the prison barber.

Speaking in general terms of the whole body all types of character were represented. Some when in funds liked to pose as dandies with fine linen, smart shoes or rope sandals tied with ribbons and coloured sashes (fajas); others, the larger number, were coarse and brutal ruffians, without private means, or too idle to acquire them by the labour of their hands, much given to drunkenness and very quarrelsome in their cups. The attitude of most convicts is mute irritation against everyone, but they especially hate their warders and superiors; they are surly and forbidding in manner, silent as to their past, little disposed to talk of their criminal adventures. Yet they display the most contradictory traits. Even when they have been guilty of the most horrible misdeeds they often show a calm, innocent face and are little vexed by conscience. One who was noted for his submissive demeanour and who in any trouble always sided with authority, was a parricide who had killed his father under the most revolting conditions.

This youth, barely of age at the time of his crime, had sought his father's consent to his marriage with an unworthy character, and when refused, he retaliated by beating in his parent's brain with a pickaxe. The fit of homicidal fury which possessed him drove him to kill his father's donkey also and the dog which had been at his heels. Then, having satiated his rage, he went home seemingly undisturbed, and made some paltry excuse for his father's absence. When the corpse was found he was arrested on suspicion, but for want of more than circumstantial evidence escaped the garrote, and was sent to Ceuta

for life. Yet this miscreant betrayed no outward
sign of the horrible passions that sometimes dominated him, but was always placid and of an engag-
ing countenance. He was lamblike in his demeanour, most attentive to his religious duties, never
missed a mass or failed to confess. He was devoted
to children and his greatest pleasure was to fondle
the baby child of one of the warders which he carried about in his arms in the streets of Ceuta. He
seemed absolutely callous and insensible to the prick-
ings of conscience, but he showed in two ways that
he was consumed with remorse. When any reference was made to his crime, at the slightest hint or
the vaguest question, a fierce look came into his eyes,
his mouth closed, his hand sought his knife and he
was ready to attempt some fresh act of violence. The
other sign of his mental distress was that he seldom
slept and never soundly or for long, and his nights
were disturbed with groans, deep sighs, even yells of
despair. Yet his general health was good, he ate
with appetite, maintained his strength well, and
there was no apparent mental failure. But he was
no doubt mad and under a more intelligent system
of jurisprudence he would have been relegated to a
criminal lunatic asylum. There is no record however that at Ceuta he had been seized again by homicidal mania.

There were many other types of murderers in
Ceuta. The husbands who had killed their wives
formed a distinct group. Jealousy because of real

or fancied injury led to the vindictive thirst for revenge and this was more frequently found in the peasant than in the higher and better educated classes. Death had been inflicted in most cases by violence, but one aggrieved Othello chose poison, rejoicing in the acute suffering produced by arsenic. Another, who was half a Frenchman, adopted the French method of dismemberment, and to dispose of the damning evidence of the corpse, cut it up into small pieces and distributed them far and wide, but could not hide them effectually. Extenuating circumstances were allowed him and he went to Ceuta, where he is said to have lived quite contentedly, never regretting the savage act that had avenged his dishonour and made him a widower.

Ceuta made its own murderers. Duels to the death were of constant occurrence as elsewhere, and the authorities rarely interfered even when fatal consequences ensued. On this point Relosillas says: " During my stay of fourteen months in Ceuta hardly an hour passed without a serious quarrel, not a day when some one was not wounded, not a week without a violent death in the *Cuartel Principal*. These troubles were due invariably to the same causes, the admission of *aguardiente* and the facility with which knives and lethal weapons could be obtained — points already noted and discussed at the beginning of this chapter. The drink was always on tap, as it could be introduced without difficulty through the dishonesty of the warders and the unlimited traffic with the townspeople. The weapons were never wanting, as it was impossible to check their presence, for no convict would be without his long sharp knife ready for instant use.

CHAPTER IX

BRIGANDS AND BRIGANDAGE

Disordered state of Spain at the accession of Isabella — Brigandage raised into an organised system by lawless nobility and rebels — The revival of the Santa Hermandad or Holy Brotherhood — This institution revived again in the 19th century under the name of "Migueletes" — Attack on the mail coach outside Madrid — The famous brigand José Maria — His daring robberies in the Serrania — His early life — English officers from Gibraltar captured and held to ransom — Beloved and venerated by the peasants — In 1833 appointed an officer of the Migueletes — Brigandage not extinct in Spain — Don Julian de Zugasti appointed governor of Cordova — Methods of procedure — The famous robber Vizco el Borje — His seizure of Don Pedro de M. — Enormous ransom extorted — Agua Dulce.

BRIGANDAGE, the form of organised highway robbery practised by bands of thieves in countries where roads are long and lonely and imperfectly guarded, has been always popular with the Latin races. It suited the tastes and temperament of reckless people who defied the law and laughed at the attempt to protect defenceless wayfarers. Their activity was stimulated by the long wastes of rugged country that separated the towns, giving harbourage and security to the robbers who issued forth to prey upon travellers and easily retired to their rocky fastnesses and escaped pursuit. These Ishmaelites have been especially active in Spain and Italy and the aggressive spirit that moved them is not yet entirely extinct. More settled government has produced a more effective police in these latter days, but acts of brigandage in its latest development, that of " holding up " modern means of conveyance, express trains, bicycles and motor cars, have occurred, and may be reasonably expected to increase.

Brigandage is as old as the hills in Spain and some of its earliest phases are well worth describing before they are forgotten or replaced by newer processes. We may look back and gather some idea of those early days in Spain.

When Isabella, the Catholic, ascended the throne of Castile, she was called upon to govern a country profoundly demoralised, infested with evil doers and dominated by a turbulent and vicious nobility. The throne was an object of contempt, the treasury empty, the people poverty stricken, and the princes of the Church rebellious and rejoicing in large revenues. A lawless aristocracy hungry for independent authority were fighting for their own lands or conspiring secretly to overawe the Crown. Titled alcaldes, traitors and rebels, openly raised brigandage into a system, exacted tribute by blackmail from the lower classes, and made unceasing war upon the higher. Within the kingdom a rival pretender aimed at the Crown. One near neighbour, Al-

fonso V of Portugal, menaced the peace of the country and kept an army on the frontier; another,
Louis XI of France, crafty and unscrupulous, constantly threatened war and held his army in Gui-
puscoa.

In a few short years the whole aspect of the country was changed.   Isabella brought her rebellious
nobles to their knees, all of them asking pardon and
promising allegiance; the French army withdrew
hastily to France; the Portuguese was defeated and
expelled; the claimant to the throne was imprisoned
and numbers of high-born criminals suffered on the
scaffold. The great ecclesiastics disgorged much of
their wealth to buy forgiveness, the robber haunts
were attacked and destroyed, the high-roads became
perfectly safe, thieves and highwaymen took to honest labour. Now the revenue was largely improved,
the law was respected, crime was actively pursued
and rigorously punished. But for the terrors and
cruelties practised by the Inquisition, Spain would
have enjoyed unbroken domestic peace and all the
benefits accruing from general good government.
These satisfactory results were largely achieved by
the excellent police organised by Isabella and her
husband, Ferdinand. The revival and consolidation
of the " Santa Hermandad " or Holy Brotherhood
which had always existed in the country districts to
secure peace and tranquillity, but heretofore wield-
ing smaller powers, worked wonders. A compre-
hensive system was now introduced by which all

parts were patrolled by well-armed guardians of the law, mounted and on foot, who checked, prevented or punished misdeeds. In every collection of thirty houses or more two officials were appointed to deal with all offenders according to a strict code. Every thief when taken was punished with fine, flogging and exile, in penalties proportioned to the amount stolen. For more heinous offences his ears were cut off and he got a hundred lashes, or yet again one of his feet was amputated and he was peremptorily forbidden to ride on a horse or mule at peril of his life. A sentence of death was carried out by shooting with arrows.

This ancient Hermandad was at one time revived in the *Migueletes,* a body of men organised early in the nineteenth century to act as escorts to private travellers, as the regular mails and diligences were under the protection of troops provided by the Government. The *Migueletes* were a semi-military force composed of picked youths of courageous conduct, wearing uniform and armed with a short gun, with a sword, a single pistol and carrying a cord by which to secure their prisoners. The *Migueletes* took their name from one Miguel de Pratz, who had been a lieutenant of Caesar Borgia. They were often recruited from the robbers who were offered service as a condition of pardon when captured, and afterwards behaved admirably. No one with an escort of ten or twelve *Migueletes* need fear attack.

The mail coach was sometimes attacked, and on

one occasion was stopped at Almuwadiel outside
Madrid. It carried several passengers, among
others an Englishman, a German artist and a Spaniard. At the first appearance of the brigands, the
guard threw himself on the ground with his face in
the mud and the postillions did the same. When
summoned to deliver up their possessions, the Englishman gave up his well filled purse and was warmly
thanked; the German artist would have been ill-
treated as a punishment for his empty pockets, but
was spared when his poverty was explained; the
Spaniard was caught attempting to conceal his valuables in the carriage lining and narrowly escaped a
beating. The coach was at last permitted to proceed
and at parting the leader of the band shook hands
with the Englishman and said he was a real gentleman, the German was ignored and the Spaniard was
sharply taken to task for his attempted " fraud."

To this period (1825-35) belongs the famous
brigand, José Maria, the Spanish Fra Diavolo,
whose name is still remembered in the " Serrania "
or mountain country of Ronda and throughout
Southern Andalusia, for his daring robberies and
continual defiance of the authorities. A " pass " or
safe conduct granted by him was a better protection
than any official escort. So great was his power
that he was known by the proud title of " El Señor
del Campo " (the lord of the country), and he ruled
more absolutely in Andalusia than King Ferdinand
in Spain. Travellers paid him a head tax, black-

mail was levied on all public conveyances and, as
has been said, he issued passports at a price to all
who chose to pay for his protection. Strong bodies
of troops were sent against him, but he managed
always to elude or oppose them successfully.

José Maria started in life as a small cultivator in a
village near Antequera, but, unable to earn a decent
living, he took to the more profitable business of
smuggling, a profession greatly honoured and esteemed in Spain. In one of his operations he was
drawn into an affray with the soldiers and unfor-
tunately shot and killed one of them. He at once
fled to the mountains, where he was soon surrounded
by other no less reckless companions, all of them
outlaws like himself, and became the chief and
centre of the band which soon spread terror throughout Southern Spain. His headquarters were in the
rugged and lofty mountain district of Ronda near
the little town of Grazalema, but he was ubiquitous
in his rapid movements and traversed the whole of
Andalusia. A story is preserved of an English
nobleman who travelled to Spain for the express
purpose of making his acquaintance but long sought
him in vain in his favourite haunts and much disap-
pointed retraced his steps to Madrid. But on the
road between Carmona and Ecija [1] he had the ques-

---

[1] This town of Ecija is renowned in the history of Spanish
brigandage as the home of the " Seven Sons of Ecija," a
very daring and dangerous band whose achievements have
been told by the Spanish novelist, Fernandez y Gonzalez.

tionable good fortune to meet José Maria in person,
who thanked him courteously for the compliment he
had paid him in seeking an interview, in return for
which he proceeded to relieve his lordship of his
valuables and his baggage so that he might continue
his journey without encumbrance. He had many
ways of levying contributions. One was to send
a messenger to some landed proprietor, demanding
a large sum of money, and declaring that if it was
not paid he would swoop down to lay waste his
lands and burn his house over his head. Another
plan was to take post with his gang, all of them well
mounted and fully armed, on the highroad just outside some populous city, and "hold up" every one
who passed in or out, seizing all ready money and
carrying off to some secret fastness all persons
known to possess means.

English officers, part of the garrison of the Rock
of Gibraltar, did not escape the exactions of José
Maria. Once a shooting party in the woods near
Gibraltar was suddenly attacked and captured, but
after the first surprise they showed fight and a brig-
and was wounded. The lives of all of them were in
danger but were saved on the persuasion of José
Maria that they would be more valuable as prisoners for whom a large ransom would be obtained
than as corpses. One of the party was accordingly
sent to the Rock to procure the money while the
rest were detained as hostages for his return at a
certain hour the next day. The messenger was

warned that if a rescue was attempted, the whole of the prisoners would be instantly massacred. He reached the Rock after gunfire, but the gates were presently especially opened to admit him, the money was collected, not without difficulty, and was conveyed to the brigands in sufficient time to secure the release of the captives. For some time later English officers were forbidden to go into Spain except in sufficient numbers to set the brigands at defiance. In quite recent years (1871) two gentlemen, natives of the Rock, were carried off and detained until a large ransom was paid.

José Maria dominated the country for nearly ten years. The secret of his long continued impunity may be traced to the fact that many of the local authorities, influenced either by fear or interest, were in collusion with him, and that the peasantry all wished him success; for, as he never oppressed them, but assisted and protected their smuggling transactions in which they are nearly all, in one way or other, engaged by opposing the regular troops, he was greatly beloved and venerated. He was in fact regarded as a hero; for such a life, wild and adventurous, where there is plenty of plunder and no laborious duty, has wondrous charms in the eyes of the lower Andalusians, by whom the laws of *meum* and *tuum* have never been well understood. How long José might have continued in power it is impossible to say, but like some other great personages he chose to abdicate. In 1833, he made his own

terms with the Queen's government, agreeing to
break up his band on condition of receiving an *in-
dulto,* or pardon for all past offences, and a salaried
appointment as an officer of Migueletes, or " police."
He did not long exercise this honest calling, for
soon after, when attempting to secure some of his
former comrades who had taken refuge in a farm-
house, he was shot dead as he burst open the door.

With all his bad qualities, José had some of a
redeeming character. Among these were his kindness to his female prisoners, his generosity to the
poor, and his forbearance, for he frequently re-
strained his troop from acts of violence, and displayed on occasions a certain chivalrous nobility of
character, hardly to be expected from a robber. In
person he was very small, scarcely more than five
feet in height, with bowed legs; but he was stout,
strong and active and made amends in boldness, determination and talent for his physical deficiencies.
His success and the long continued control which he
exercised over the lawless fellows who composed his
band proved that he possessed the difficult art of
command. His courage indeed was proverbial. As
an instance of it, it is reported that he once ventured
into the presence of the Prime Minister at Madrid
and dared to beard him in his own house.

Brigandage has not wholly disappeared in Spain
although it no longer exists on the grand scale of
former days when the mountain passes and lesser
highways were infested by robber bands led by dar-

ing and unscrupulous chiefs who stopped travellers, blackmailed landed proprietors and carried off country folk whom they held to ransom often for considerable sums. To-day, if the knights of the road are still to be met with occasionally, they are for the most part paltry pilferers bent on stealing small sums from the poorer folk returning from market, or in rare cases holding up some solitary vehicle and its defenceless passengers. These are of the type of the old fashioned *salteadores* or " jumpers," so named because they jumped out from behind a rock and dropped suddenly on their prey with the old peremptory summons of *" Boca abajo! " " Boca à tierra! "* " Faces down! Mouth to the ground! " The cry may still be heard, and it means mischief when backed as of old by the muzzle of a gun protruding from the bushes in some narrow pass or defile. They are courageous too, these Spanish road agents, ready to fight at need as well as to rob, to overbear resistance and to meet the officers of the law with their own weapons. A story is told of one daring ruffian, Rullo de Zancayro, who, in 1859, murdered the alcalde of his village and was followed by two *guardias civiles*. At the end of a long chase they went too near some brushwood, when one was shot dead and the fugitive made good his escape.

In the year 1870 brigandage was general throughout Spain, but the heart and centre of it was the province of Andalusia, with branches and ramifications everywhere, spreading dismay and apprehension among all peaceable people. This was in the interregnum that followed the revolution which drove Queen Isabella from the throne. There was safety for no one. Respectable landowners dared not visit nor reside upon their estates for fear of attack, dreading robbery with violence or seizure of their persons, and they constantly received threatening letters demanding the purchase of immunity on the payment of considerable sums. The roads were more than ever insecure, trains and diligences were repeatedly held up, and small parties of travellers or solitary wayfarers were certain to be laid under contribution. It was claimed that the *guardias civiles,* the fine rural police, were no longer active but were diverted from their legitimate duties by political party leaders in power. So many bitter complaints, so many indignant demands for protection, reached the central government in Madrid, that the authorities resolved to put down brigandage with a strong hand. A new governor of Cordova was appointed, a man of vigour and determination, armed with full powers to purge the province of its desperadoes.

The choice fell upon Don Julian de Zugasti y Saenz, who had been a member of the Cortes and employed as civil administrator, first as governor of Teruel, where he had restored order in a period of grave disorder, and at Burgos, where he had laid bare a formidable conspiracy against the government. When Zugasti undertook the task, it was high time to adopt energetic measures. There was no security for life or property as robberies on a large scale were perpetrated both in town and country. Well-to-do citizens were seized in the public streets and carried off to sequestration; farmers and cultivators were compelled to share their produce, their harvests, and their herds with the brigands who swooped down on them; the police were impotent or too much owerawed to interfere in the interest of honest folk. The prevailing anarchy and widespread lawlessness were a disgrace to any country that called itself civilised. Zugasti did a great work in restoring order and giving security to the disturbed districts. The whole story is told at some length in his book on " Bandolerismo," [1] which deals with brigandage in Spain from its very beginnings, describing the principal feats of the banditti.

At the outset he was faced with a most difficult situation. Crimes in great number had been committed with impunity. Many of their perpetrators were wholly hidden from the authorities, while others were perfectly well known. A crowd of spies were ever on the watch and ready, whether from greed or to curry favour, with abundant information of openings that offered for attempts at crime. On the other hand the *guardias civiles* were greatly discouraged and far too weak in numbers for the

[1] "Bandolerismo estudo social y memorias historicas," by Don Julian de Zugasti. Madrid, 1876.

onerous duties they were expected to perform.
Judges were dishonest and had been known to accept bribes, the ordinary police were torpid, nearly
useless and generally despised. A complete reform
in the administration of justice was a crying need,
as the power and authority of the law were com-
pletely broken down.

The new governor was helpless and handicapped
on every side. His representations to the government for support were but coldly received and he
had to rely on such scanty means as he had at hand.
He looked carefully into the character of all police
employés and dismissed all of doubtful reputation.
He established a system of supplying the *guardias
civiles* at all stations with photographs of criminals
at large whom they could identify and arrest, and
insisted on strictly revising the permits issued to
carry arms, allowing none but respectable persons
to do so. The prohibition was extended to all kinds
of knives, many of them murderous weapons of the
well known type. The quarters of all evil doers
he heard of were broken up, including the farm
which had come to be called Ceuta because it har-
boured a mob of ex-convicts, escaped prisoners who
were eager to resume their depredations by joining
themselves to the plans and projects of others.

These active measures were bitterly resented and
vigorously resisted by all evil doers, who went so
far as to seek the removal of the governor, and it
was falsely announced in more than one newspaper

that he had sent in his resignation. The disastrous consequence was the immediate revival of brigandage in various forms. Horses and cattle were once more stolen in the open country and a house in the town of Estado was broken into and a large amount in cash and securities with much valuable jewelry was seized. At the same time ten prisoners escaped in a body from the gaol of that city. On the highroad between Posadas and Villaviciosa, seven armed men robbed nineteen travellers, and a party had the audacity to carry off a child of nine and hold him to ransom. The police and well-disposed people were greatly disheartened, the *guardias civiles,* which had done excellent service in capturing more than a hundred prisoners in a short time, slackened in their endeavours, while the municipal police, which had forty captures to its credit, also held their hand. The whole situation was greatly aggravated and crime gained the ascendancy. But Zugasti rose to the occasion, publicly denied the report of his resignation; the government published a complimentary decree commending his conduct, and his pursuit of wrong doers was continued with renewed energy. Naturally he incurred the bitterest hostility and went constantly in danger of his life. He received anonymous letters containing the most bloodthirsty threats and was warned by his friends that they could not possibly support or protect him. Undeterred he held his way, bravely and wisely organised an association akin to the " Regulators " of the wild days in the Western States of the United States to patrol the country and insure the general safety, and employed a large force of secret police agents to perambulate the country, keeping close watch upon suspicious persons, travelling by all trains, patrolling all roads, visiting taverns in low quarters, entering the prisons in disguise and gaining the confidence of the fellow prisoners. Zugasti himself spent long periods in the various gaols, observing, investigating and interviewing notable offenders.

The thoroughness of his proceedings might be gathered from the choice he made of his agents. One of the most useful was an idiot boy, whose weak-mindedness was relieved by some glimmerings of sense and who passed entirely unsuspected by those upon whom he spied. His foolish talk and silly ways gained him ready admission into cafés and clubs, where he was laughed at and treated as a butt upon whom food, drink and unlimited cigars were generously bestowed. He had the gift of remaining wide awake while seeming to be sound asleep, his ears ever on the stretch to pick up compromising facts which were openly mentioned before him. He had also a prodigious memory and seldom forgot what he heard, storing up everything to be produced later when he attended upon the governor. In this way Zugasti often heard of crimes almost as soon as they were planned, and could hunt up their perpetrators without delay. On one occasion a mysterious crime was unravelled by placing the idiot in the same cell with two of the suspected actors, who entirely believed in the imbecility of their cell companion and unguardedly revealed the true inwardness of the whole affair.

The *ladron en grande,* the " robber chief " at the head of a numerous band, is still to be met with, although rarely representing the type of the famous José Maria. These leaders rose to the command of their lawless fellows by force of superior will, and they were unhesitatingly obeyed and followed with reckless devotion in the constant commission of crime. One or two noted specimens have survived till to-day and some account of them may be extracted from recent records.

Vizco el Borje was long a terror to the peaceable people in northern Andalusia. He was originally an officer of *carabineros,* the " custom house " regiment of Spain, but had been, in his own judgment, unjustly dismissed and found himself deprived of the means of subsistence. Falling lower and lower, step by step he became an outcast, an Ishmaelite consumed with an intense hatred of all social arrangements, with his hand against every man. He began business as a smuggler and soon took to worse, following the Spanish proverb: —

> "De contrabandista e ladron
> No haymas que un escalon."

" There is only one short step from smuggler to thief," and Vizco quickly crossed the narrow space and became a notorious criminal. He carried on the war against law and order with constantly increasing recklessness and more and more daring outrages. His strong personal character, his iron will, his unbounded courage and boldness gave him a great ascendancy over the men who collected around him and who served him with the greatest loyalty and unstinting effort. One of his exploits may be quoted at some length as exhibiting his methods and the success that generally attended them.

A certain landowner, Don Pedro de M——, whose estates were in the neighbourhood of the mountain village of Zahrita, was in the habit of providing bulls free of charge for the amusement of the villagers, at the annual festival of their patron saint. Amateur bull fighters are always to be found to take part in the performance of a *novillos,* or game with young bulls. Don Pedro like many of his class was also an *aficionado,* an amateur devoted to bull fighting, and he loved to pick out himself the animals he gave from his herds, trying first their temper and their aptitude for the so-called sport of *tauromaquia.* He was thus engaged, assisted by his steward and a herdsman, and had dismounted with the steward to walk round the herd, when the ominous cry was raised, " *Boca abajo!* " and they found themselves covered by the rifles of three brigands who had crept upon them unobserved. Resistance was hopeless, though they also were armed, for their guns hung at the saddles of their horses, which they led at the full length of their reins, and to have made any hostile move would have drawn down a murderous fire. The chance soon passed, for one of the robbers quickly took possession of both horses and guns. The seizure was complete and the captors proceeded to carry off their prize.

All remounted by order of the chief of the band, who took the lead, and the party started in single file along the narrow mountain path, an armed escort bringing up the rear. They made straight for the upper sierra, avoiding the frequented track until they reached a dense thicket, where a halt was called and a scout sent on ahead. After an interchange of whistled signals, nine other horsemen rode up, the two prisoners were ordered to dismount, their eyes closely bandaged, and they were warned that their lives depended upon their implicit obedience to the orders they received. Then the march was resumed. The road led constantly upward, becoming more and more rugged and precipitous till from the utter absence of brushwood and the stumbling of their horses they knew that they were climbing through a mountainous region. Another halt was called, all again dismounted, and the prisoners were led on foot along a narrow passage, that from the echoing sounds and the closeness of the air evidently penetrated far into the hill. It opened presently into an extensive cavern, probably the long-abandoned workings of some ancient Roman

mine. Here their bandages were removed and Don
Pedro saw that he was in the presence of the three
bandits who had first made him prisoner. The
cave contained nothing but a few empty boxes, on
one of which was a light, a flickering wick in a sau-
cerful of oil. Another box was offered Don Pedro
as a seat, writing materials were produced and he
was desired to write from dictation as follows: —

"DEAR FATHER, I am in the power of the ' Se-
questradores,' who make good plans and bind fast.
It is madness to put the government on their track
— they will escape and you will lose your son. Your
secrecy and your money can at once free me. You
can send the silver by Diego our steward, who is
the bearer of this. Let him appear on the mountain between Grazalema and El Bosque, riding a
white donkey and bringing ten thousand dollars."

Here the prisoner stopped short and point blank
refused to demand so large a sum, declaring that
to pay it his brothers would be robbed of their patrimony and that he had no right to ask even when
his life was at stake for more than his individual
share as one member of a large family. It was a
fair argument and he held out so staunchly that the
brigand was pleased to reduce the demand to six
thousand dollars. The letter conveying these terms
was then completed, signed and delivered to Diego,
who was told to make the best of his way to Xeres,

and as dawn had now broken he had no difficulty in finding the road.

Don Pedro was hospitably entertained. A wine skin (*borracha*) was broached and a plentiful supper laid out. The day was spent in sleep, but at nightfall the march was resumed. The prisoner was once more blindfolded, the weary pilgrimage, halting by day, travelling by night for three nights in succession, was resumed. On one occasion he seemed near rescue. A cry of " Civiles! Civiles! " was raised, an alarm of the near approach of the much dreaded *guardias civiles*. Orders were promptly issued to prepare for action. The brigands closed their ranks, sent their prisoner to the rear and took post to open fire. In the confusion Don Pedro, keenly alert for the deliverance that seemed so near, managed to lift the bandage over his eyes sufficiently to peep around. The party stood on a narrow ledge of the mountain side, straight cliff above, sheer drop below: movement forward or back was alone feasible. Meanwhile the increasing clatter of hoofs betrayed the enemy's approach, nearer and nearer, and the brigands barring the narrow road hoped to take them at a disadvantage and, after shooting them down, make good their retreat. But the sight of the first horse showed that it had been a false alarm. These were not " *Civiles* " but " *Contrabandistas*," smugglers not policemen, friends not foes. A long train of animals, heavily laden with goods that had paid no duty, were being

guided across the mountains. Don Pedro's hopes
were crushed out of him when he heard the interchange of friendly greetings: *"Muy buenas
noches!"* on one side and *"Vayan ustedes con
Dios,"* on the other; "Good night!" and "Go in
God's keeping," and room was made by the robbers
for the safe passage of the smuggling train.

On the third day news came that the authorities
were on the alert and it would be unsafe to meet
the messenger returning on his white donkey. Another tryst was therefore appointed. Don Pedro's
father was desired to send half the whole sum demanded to Grazalema and the other half was carried by a man on the white donkey to a lonely spot
among the hills. The father started in person on
the long ride from Xeres to Grazalema weighted
with three thousand dollars in cash, reached his des-
tination safely but remained there for a couple of
days tortured with suspense. On the third morning he was approached by a man leading a pony
laden with rolls of the rough brown cloth manufactured in Grazalema, who said under his breath as
he passed, "Follow me.". The peddler led the way
to a small draper's shop where the same cloth was
exposed for sale and, dismounting, passed into the
back premises, where another man, also a peddler,
was seated waiting. This was Vizco el Borje himself, who at once asked for the money, producing
Don Pedro's pencil case as his credentials. The dollars had been sewn for security into the pack saddle

of the pony which had brought the old man, and they were extracted, counted and handed over. Vizco forthwith climbed on top of the pile of cloth carried by his own mount and rode boldly out of the town.

Meanwhile Diego, the steward on the white donkey, with the remaining three thousand dollars patiently hung about the mountain lair to which he had been directed, and at last encountered a goatherd at the entrance of the village, who told him to ride on till he met a woman dressed in black seated by the side of a well. " She will ask you the time, and you will answer twelve o'clock, at which she will guide you to the spot where you are expected." It was a cavern in the hill and he was met there by his young master Don Pedro safe and sound. The money was handed over, but no release was permitted until news came of the delivery of the other half, when the prisoners were guided to a path familiar to them and they were free to return home. Next evening they rode into Xeres after a captivity of fifteen days.

The end of Vizco el Borje was such as might be expected. He was shot down by the *guardias civiles*. For a long time he carried his life in his hands and had many hairbreadth escapes, saved always by his fine pluck and resourcefulness. At last the authorities had positive information of his whereabouts, gained through treachery, and he was surrendered. He made a gallant defence, but his retreat was cut off and he was soon overpowered. When he fell his body had been pierced by five rifle bullets.

Another type of brigand was Agua Dulce, who worked on a much smaller scale, but was long a terror in the neighbourhood of Xeres. He was a mean, contemptible ruffian who preyed upon charcoal burners, poor travellers, carriers and workmen returning home with their hard earned wages. He had one narrow escape. After securing an unusually large sum, the equivalent of £600, all in small coins, he was caught dividing these with two accomplices in a wine shop. His arrest and imprisonment followed. When called upon to account for his possession of the gold, Agua Dulce explained that he had got it in the course of a business transaction in Seville and was removed to that city for trial, where he was acquitted, although little doubt was entertained of his guilt.

For years he continued his depredations, committing for the most part small thefts and petty larcenies. Now and again he made bold coups, as when, under threat of damaging a herd of valuable mares, he extorted three thousand dollars from a lady who raised horses. He levied a thousand dollars on another landowner by using the same menace and a third gentleman, who had stoutly refused to be blackmailed and who owned a large drove of donkeys, found them all with their throats cut lying by the high road. When his misdeeds became too numerous to be borne the municipal guard of Gorez swore to put an end to him. A hot pursuit was organised and he was found at a ford near a wood belonging to the Duke of San Lorenzo, where he was caught hiding among the trees. Two guards opened fire, which was returned, with the result that one guard was killed and one robber. Agua Dulce, who was still alive, got into the covert, and shots were again and again exchanged, ending in the destruction of the brigand.

A later affair with brigands occurred at Gibraltar in 1870, when two gentlemen, natives of the Rock, much given to hunting and taking long rides in the neighbourhood, were waylaid and made prisoners. They were carried off to a lonely house in the hills near Ronda and detained for ransom, which was advanced by the British government through the governor of the fortress of Gibraltar, and eventually repaid by the Spanish authorities. After the money had been paid over the *guardias civiles* intercepted the robbers and shot them down.

CHAPTER X

A BRIGHT PAGE IN PRISON HISTORY

Wonderful results achieved by Colonel Montesinos in the presidio at Valencia — Montesinos repairs and reconstructs the prison with convict labour — His system of treatment — Period — Marvellous success in reforming criminals — Convicts entrusted with confidential despatches in civil war — Armed to resist attack on the prison by insurgents — Employed to hunt down brigands — Movement towards prison reform in 1844 — Three new model prisons planned for Madrid — Executions — The "garrote" — Account of the trial and execution of José de Rojas — The condemned cell at the Saladero — An Englishman's description of a Spanish execution.

THE reader who has followed this detailed description of Spanish penal methods has realised the hideous shortcomings of Spanish prisons, the horrible practices so constantly prevailing within the walls, the apparently incurable nature of the criminals who regularly fill them, and he might reasonably doubt that definite and substantial amendment was possible. Yet the contrary is true and to the most marked and astonishing degree if we are to believe the facts on record. In one instance the personal character of one man, backed by his unshaken determination and the exercise of a resolute and inflexible will, brought a large mass of convicts into an admirable condition of self-control and good behaviour. The story reads like a fairy tale, as set forth in contemporary chronicles. One of the most interesting accounts is to be found in a book of travels entitled " Spain as It Is," by a Mr. Hoskins, in which he gives his personal observations of the results achieved in the prison at Valencia by the enlightened administration of its Governor, Colonel Montesinos. A brief account of the man himself should precede our appreciation of his work.

Montesinos was a soldier, trained to arms, whose education and experience were entirely military. He had no previous acquaintance with or insight into prison systems, although he had travelled far and wide in many countries. He had never visited or inspected their penal establishments nor had he penetrated into any single prison in his native Spain. He served in the Spanish army, beginning as a cadet at fourteen, was actively engaged in the war of Independence, and was carried off as a prisoner into France. When set free at the conclusion of peace, he accepted a post in the secretariat of the War Office at Madrid, where he remained for five years. Then came the political troubles which ended in the fall of the constitutional government in 1823 and the surrender of Cadiz. With many other soldiers and citizens, he left Spain and wandered through Europe and America, with no very definite idea of examining into the laws and customs of other countries, but gaining knowledge and breadth of views. On his return to Spain when close on forty years of age he was appointed governor of the convict prison in Valencia.

Montesinos entered upon his duties with a firm conviction of the paramount importance of military discipline, of that passive and unquestioning obedience to authority, the absolute surrender of individual volition, the complete subjection of the many to the single will of one superior master, which he believed to be the essence of all personal government and more particularly in a prison. To enforce such discipline was the only effectual method of securing good order and the due subordination of the rough and possibly recalcitrant elements under his command. In this he entirely succeeded and established an extraordinary influence over his charges. He became an autocrat but in the best sense; his prisoners resigned themselves submissively and unhesitatingly to his control, anxious to gain his good will by their exemplary demeanour and their unvarying desire to behave well. What he actually made of his charges, how he succeeded in changing their very natures, in transforming lawbreakers and evil doers into honest, trustworthy persons, successfully restraining their evil instincts, will be best realised by a few strange facts which, if not positively vouched for, would be considered beyond belief. But before relating these marvellous results it will be well to describe in some detail the processes adopted by him and the principles on which he acted.

When Colonel Montesinos was appointed governor of the Valencian convent prison, it was located in an ancient mediæval edifice known as the " *Torres de Cuarte,*" two towers flanking the great gate which gave upon the suburb known as " *El Cuarte.*" This semi-ruinous building, dating from the fifteenth century, lodged about a thousand prisoners, herded together in a number of dark, dirty, ill-kept and insecure chambers, wholly unfit for human habitation. They were on several floors communicating by narrow passages and tortuous staircases, below which were deep underground cellars divided up into obscure foul dungeons, which were always humid from the infiltration from the city ditch and into which neither sunlight nor fresh air came to dry up the damp pavement and the streaming walls. Montesinos saw at once that it would be impossible to introduce reforms in such a building and he laboured hard to move into better quarters, securing at length, after a long correspondence, new quarters in the monastery of St. Augustine, which indeed was but little better. Here also the buildings had fallen into disrepair. A large part was without roof, there was little flooring, and many broken windows and decayed walls offered numerous facilities for escape. Extensive repairs were indispensable, yet funds were wanting, for the Spanish government was sorely taxed to meet the

expenses of the civil war (Carlist) now in full
swing. Nevertheless Montesinos, strenuous and
indefatigable, a host in himself, transferred his
people, a thousand convicts of dangerous character,
into their new abode and set them to work to repair
and reconstruct the old building. He meant to succeed, by drawing upon his own limitless energies,
creating means from his own native resources, and
was backed by the ready response of those he
brought under the dominion of an indomitable will.

All difficulties yielded before his intense spirit.
He was the very incarnation of activity and it was
enough to look at him to be spurred on to assiduous
effort. His personal traits and their effect upon his
surroundings are thus described by his biographer,
Vincente Boix, — " There can be no doubt that his
martial air, his tall figure and the look in his face,
a mixture of imperious command with great kindliness and shrewd appreciation of willing effort, had
a marked effect upon his people, and convicts who
had been once coerced and driven by the fear of
punishment yielded much more readily to his moral
force. His obvious determination and strength of
character got more out of them than threats or penalties, although, if needs were, he was ready enough
to appeal to the strong arm. They acknowledged
his superiority, and rough undisciplined men, quite
capable of rising against authority when unchecked
or weakly held, succumbed to his lightest word like
children to their father. They yielded even against

the grain absolute compliance to his lightest wish without needing a sharp look or a cross word."

It will be interesting to follow Montesinos' procedure. Under his system the treatment was progressive and divided into three periods; first, that of chains; second, that of labour; and third, that of conditional liberation. This arrangement is in some respects akin to that generally known as the "Irish" system as practised many years ago with conspicuous success.

(1) The wearing of irons at that time was general in Spain, although now the practice has fallen into disuse. With Montesinos the rule was to impose irons of varying weight graduated to the length of sentence. A two years' man carried them of four pounds' weight; a four years' man of six pounds, while between six and eight years they were of eight pounds. They consisted of a single chain fastened to a fetter on the right ankle, while the other end was attached to a waist belt, a method supposed to cause no great inconvenience. With Montesinos the period of wearing them was of short duration. It terminated on the day that the convict petitioned for regular employment, for on first reception, after having entered the first courtyard, which was kept bright with garden flowers and the songs of many birds in cages hanging around, the new arrival was given no work. He remained at the depot idle and silent, for no conversation was permitted, although he was associated with others,

and if he put a question to a neighbour he got no reply. Weariness and boredom soon supervened in this period of first probation and the convict was keen to pass on. He appealed to his officer, who told him to seek employment at some trade. " I know none." " Then learn one, you cannot get quit of your irons in any other way." If the convict hesitated he was left studiously to himself, unhappy and ashamed, for his condition was deemed disgraceful. He could not hold his head up, for a wide gulf separated him from others who had escaped the chain. He was a marked man, shunned and sneered at, and was required to work from the second day at ignominious and humiliating labour, such as sweeping, cleaning, and so forth. They were the helots and scavengers of the prison. Their lot was the more unbearable because they were debarred from many privileges conferred on those who were at regular labour, and who were earning wages to spend in part upon themselves. These regular labourers might buy toothsome food and cigars, the delight of every Spaniard's heart. Meanwhile the governor had been watching him closely, noting his disposition and whether or not he was desirous of taking up work which was so much to his advantage and of which he would be speedily deprived unless he applied himself to it with zeal and unflagging industry.

(2) A wide choice of labour obtained in Valencia. Trades and handicrafts were varied and

numerous. Carpenters, turners, saddlers, shoe-makers, fanmakers, workers with esparto grass, weavers of palm straw hats, silk spinners, tailors, basket makers, were all represented, and the total was some forty trades, with seven hundred artisans. To-day there would be nothing remarkable in this industrial activity, which may be seen in well governed prisons, but in Valencia at that date (1835-40) it was a novelty due very largely to Montesinos' initiative, and he could boast that out of three thousand convicts, barely a fourth left prison without having acquired some smattering of a trade. Stress must not be laid upon the exact amount of skill possessed by these prison taught artisans, and it is to be feared that it was no more thorough than in these latter days of ours, when the same principles as those of Montesinos have actuated prison administration. This is the crux of the system of prison instruction. It cannot be expected to turn out workmen sufficiently well trained and expert to go out into the open labour market, so generally overcrowded, and compete for wages against the free labourer who has had the benefit of full apprenticeship. Adults cannot easily acquire knowledge and dexterity in the use of tools, and inevitable waste of materials accompanies the experiments made by unskilled hands. We have no record of how far these drawbacks affected Montesinos' well-meant practice.

(3) We have no facts to show how far the third

period, that of conditional liberation, was successful at Valencia. There is no possibility of knowing
definitely whether it was really tried or went beyond the enunciation of the theory so long in advance of our modern practice. It is little likely,
however, that the effective and elaborate method of
police supervision on which it is absolutely dependent was in existence or even understood in Spain
in the days of Montesinos.

No permanent results seemed to have been
achieved by the Montesinos system. There is no
record that it survived the man who created it or
that the government sought to extend the admirable
principles on which it rested. It was essentially a
one man system, depending entirely for success on
the personal qualities of the individual called upon
to carry it out. Montesinos was not, however, singular in his remarkable achievement. The German
Obermaier did much the same in the prison of Kai-
serslautern, and Captain Maconochie in Norfolk
Island exercised a notable mastery over the Australian convicts. The effects produced by Montesinos were little less than phenomenal. He so developed the probity of his convicts that he could
rely implicitly upon their honesty and good faith.
During the civil war he sent them with confidential
despatches to commanders in the field and never had
cause to regret the trust placed in them. They were
sent out as scouts seeking information of the
enemy's movements and brought in news with

punctuality and despatch. A message was brought one day to the governor directing him to send a clerk to fetch a thousand dollars from the provincial Treasury. Montesinos forthwith summoned one of his convicts and despatched him, carrying with him the receipt for the money. Within half an hour the man returned with the dollars. Whenever a convict escaped from the presidio, a rare occurrence indeed, other convicts were despatched in pursuit and seldom failed to bring in the fugitive.

At one time the Spanish government decided to build a new prison in the capital and to employ convict labour in the construction. The Governor of the presidio of Valencia was ordered to send up a number of prisoners, and next day at daylight they marched, taking with them a quantity of material, the whole escorted by a small body of *cabos,* " prisoner warders," and commanded by a veteran overseer. The journey was safely made to Madrid without the smallest mishap, not a sign or symptom of misbehaviour shown on the road, and the alcaldes of the towns on the route, after anticipating the worst evils, were agreeably surprised and were satisfied to lodge the travellers at night in private houses if there was no prison accommodation. A second experiment of the kind was made in the same year.

On a previous occasion Valencia was threatened by a strong force of Carlists under that distinguished Carlist general, Cabrera, and it was feared that he would capture a large body of convicts at that time employed on a new road, Las Cabrillas, a little distance from the city. There were hardly any troops in the capital except the city militia only recently organised and barely equal to the duties and dangers imposed upon them. Great fears were entertained that Cabrera would seize the convicts and incorporate with his own force. Montesinos was desired to prevent this, and he turned up in person one evening at Las Cabrillas, where he assumed command and drew off the greater number, happily escaping without attack or interference by the enemy. So loyal was the demeanour of the Valencian prisoners that under the direction of Montesinos at another time they were armed and resisted an attack made upon the gates of their convent prison by the insurgents in a rising in Valencia. The following extraordinary story is related in an official publication by the well known poet Don Ramon de Campoamor, at that time governor of the province of Valencia. A formidable band of brigands was devastating the neighbourhood of Valencia and a reign of terror prevailed. The governor sent for Colonel Montesinos and inquired whether there were any old brigands among the convicts in custody and who were willing to atone for past misdeeds by coming to the assistance of the authorities. Montesinos, who made it a rule to know all his prisoners by heart, their present dispositions, and indeed their inmost thoughts, spoke confidently of one

as quite a reformed character, and at the governor's
request entrusted him with the special mission of
clearing out the country. The convict, after receiving his instructions, went out with a sufficient escort,
hunted down the brigands, broke up their bands,
killing or capturing the whole. Here the commanding influence of Montesinos was paramount even
beyond the walls of the presidio. By the power of
his strong will he called out fine qualities and exacted loyal service from the worst materials whom
he had won to a high sense of discipline.

A minor and more sentimental instance is recorded of the confidence he could repose in his
reformed criminals. The mother of one of the convicts was at the point of death. The man was
summoned to the governor's office and informed of
her desperate condition. "Do you wish to see her
in her last moments?" asked the governor. "Can
I trust you to return if I give you permission to
leave the prison for a time?" The man much
moved solemnly promised not to misuse his liberty.
He was allowed to exchange his prison uniform for
a peasant's dress; he went without escort to his
mother's cottage, received her blessing, and went
back to durance as had been agreed.

The experience of Valencia was unique and short-
lived. A commendable effort was made to extend
the principles on which Montesinos had acted, and
decrees embodying them and recommending them
for general adoption were issued but soon became

a dead letter. Excellent in theory, their success depended entirely on the man to give them effect. A second Montesinos did not appear and Spanish prisons continued to exhibit the worst features down to the present day.

A movement towards prison reform had been commenced as early as 1844, when three new "model" prisons were planned for Madrid, but their construction was long delayed. About the same date a model convict prison was planned at Valladolid, but slow progress was made with this and with other new prisons, including that of Saragossa, and at the Casa de Galera of Alcala de Henares. A penitentiary was also projected on the island of Cabrera, opposite Cadiz. The chief effort was concentrated on the model prison of Madrid, which was undertaken in 1876 after much debate and discussion. It was to be an entirely new building, to which were devoted all the funds that might have been expended upon the impossible reform and repair of the hideous old Saladero. Several years passed before the building began, and not until 1884 did the tenants of the dismantled Saladero move into the new prison. It is for the most part on the cellular or separate system, by which each individual is held strictly apart from his fellows, according to the most modern ideas, which have claimed to have exerted a potent effect in the reformation of offenders and the diminution of crime. Nevertheless the system is still in its trial and its beneficial results are by no means universally conceded. The new prison is a very distinct improvement on the old, and the former horrors and atrocities are fast disappearing, but the secluded solitary life has its own peculiar terrors which press hardly on transgressors, with results that are very distinctly deterrent if not very largely reformatory.

What those actually subjected to the treatment feel we may read in their own effusions. The literary quality of prison writers does not rank high but they sometimes put their views forcibly. One says of the "model": — "If I leave this trying place alive I can at least declare that I have been buried underground and had made the acquaintance of the grave diggers." Another writer: — "If you wish to know what life is like here, come and take your lodging inside. They are handsome, but curious, well provided with means to drive you out of your mind. There is a water tap which overflows in drought and runs dry in wet weather; a pocket handkerchief and a towel; a plate, a basin and a wooden spoon, a broom, a dust box, one blanket and a mattress with four straws that gives you pain in every limb: many things more, but one alone much needed is absent, a rope by which you commit suicide."

It has been said that the worst use to which a man may be put is to shut him up in a prison. A still more wasteful extravagance is to put him out of the world. The penalties known to Spanish law

have been very various; there have been many
forms of imprisonment, perpetual imprisonment,
greater or less detention, exile, the application of
fetters of several sorts, handcuffs, shackles, the
guarda amigo or "holdfriend," the "persuader" or
"come along with me"; the leg irons and waist
chains of varying weights. Penal labour was enforced in *maniobras infimas* by convicts chained together on public works, fortifications, harbours and
mines. All forms of secondary punishment have
been inflicted, winding up with capital, the death
sentence inflicting the extreme penalty of the law.
This last irrevocable act does not find favour with
all Spanish legists, whose chief objection is the familiar one that when a judicial error has been committed, rectification is altogether impossible. Spain
can add one to the many well known cases such as
those of Callas and Lesurques, and it may be quoted
here as it is probably little known.

The case occurred in Seville and grew out of a
sudden quarrel in a tavern followed by a fight to the
death with knives. The combatants went on the
ground and attacked each other in the regular
fashion when one dropped to the ground mortally
wounded and the other with his second ran away.
The wounded man's second went up to see whether
his principal was dying or already dead, when he
got up and declared that he was entirely unhurt.
He had slipped upon a stone and fallen with the obviously cowardly desire to escape from his antag-

onist's attack. The second was furiously angry and
rated his man soundly. He retorted fiercely and
another quarrel and another encounter ensued, also
with knives, in which the first man again fell and
this time was killed outright, by his own second,
who at once made off. The body lay where it had
fallen until next morning, when the police found it.
The story of the original quarrel but nothing of the
second had become known, and it was naturally concluded that death had been inflicted by the first
combatant. On the face of it the evidence was con-
clusive against him, and he did not attempt to deny
the facts as they appeared when arrested and put
upon his trial. At that time the law treated homi-
cide in a duel as murder and the victim suffered the
extreme penalty without protest, believing himself
to be guilty. The truth was never known, until the
real offender, years after, confessed the part he had
played, but too late of course to prevent the judicial
murder of the innocent man. This case has naturally been added to give weight to the many powerful arguments against capital punishment.

The extreme penalty of the law is nowadays inflicted in Spain by the *garrote,* a method of strangulation by the tightening of an iron collar, the substitute for hanging introduced by King Ferdinand
VII (1820). Till then the hanging was carried
out in the clumsiest and most brutal manner. The
culprits were dragged by the executioner up the
steps of a ladder leaning against the scaffold. At

a certain height he mounted on the victim's shoulders and thus seated flung himself off with his victim underneath. As they swung to and fro the hangman's fingers were busily engaged in choking the convict so as to complete the strangulation. The *garrote* is a very simple contrivance. The condemned man sits on a stool or low seat, leaning his back against a strong, firm upright post to which an iron collar is fixed. This, when opened, encircles his neck, and is closed and tightened by a powerful screw, worked by a lever from behind. Death is instantaneous.

Public executions must prove very popular performances with a people who still revel in a bull fight and flock to look at the hairbreadth escapes of human beings from hardly undeserved death by the horns of a fierce beast tortured into madness. De Foresta, an Italian traveller,[1] tells us that never was a greater concourse seen in Madrid than that which collected in 1877 to witness the execution of two murderers, Mollo and Agullar, when it was estimated that 80,000 people were present. Ford describes an execution in Seville in 1845 when the crowd was enormous and composed largely of the lower orders, of the humbler ranks, " who hold the conventions of society very cheap and give loose rein to their morbid curiosity to behold scenes of terror, which operates powerfully on the women,

[1] La Spagna; Da Irun a Malaga, by Adolfo de Foresta, Bologna, 1879.

who seem irresistibly impelled to witness sights the most repugnant to their nature and to behold sufferings which they would most dread to undergo," and many of whom "brought in their arms young children at the beginning of life to witness its conclusion." "They desire to see how the criminal will conduct himself, they sympathise with him if he displays coolness and courage, and despise him on the least symptom of unmanliness."

Ford in his "Gatherings from Spain" gives a graphic account of the execution of a highway robber, one of the band of the famous José Maria already mentioned. The culprit, José de Rojas, was nicknamed "Veneno," poison, from his venomous qualities and had made a desperate resistance before he was finally overcome by the troops who captured him. He fell wounded with a bullet in his leg, but killed the soldier who ran forward to secure him. When in custody he turned traitor and volunteered to betray his old associates and give such information as would lead to their arrest if his own life was spared. The offer was accepted and he was sent out with a sufficient force to seize them. Such was the terror of his name that all surrendered, but not to him. On this quibble the indemnity promised him was withdrawn, he was brought to trial, condemned, and in due course executed on the Plaza San Francisco, which adjoins the prison in Seville and is commonly used for public executions.

Ford was admitted within the walls and describes

Veneno " *en capilla,*" a small room set apart as a condemned cell, the approach to which was thronged with officers, portly Franciscan friars and "members of a charitable brotherhood collecting alms from the visitors to be expended in masses for the eternal repose of the soul of the criminal. The levity of those assembled without, formed a heartless contrast with the gloom and horror of the melancholy interior of the *capilla.* At the head of the cell was placed a table with a crucifix, an image of the Virgin and two wax tapers, near which stood a silent sentinel with a drawn sword. Another soldier was stationed at the door with a fixed bayonet. In a corner of this darkened compartment lay Veneno curled up like a snake, with a striped coverlet drawn closely over his mouth, leaving visible only a head of matted locks, and a glistening dark eye rolling restlessly out of its deep socket. On being approached he sprang up and seated himself on a stool. He was almost naked, but a chaplet of beads hung across his exposed breast and contrasted with the iron chains around his limbs. . . . The expression of his face though low and vulgar was one which, once seen, was not easily forgotten. His sallow complexion appeared more cadaverous in the uncertain light and was heightened by a black unshorn beard, growing vigorously on a half-dead countenance. He appeared to be reconciled to his fate and repeated a few sentences, the teaching of the monks, as by rote. His situation was probably more painful to the spectator than himself, an indifference to death arising rather from an ignorance of its dreadful import than from high moral courage."

When Veneno came out to die he was clad in a coarse yellow baize gown, the colour which in Spain denotes the crime of murder and appropriated always to Judas Iscariot in Spanish paintings, the colour, too, of the *sanbenito* or penitential cloak worn by the victims of the Inquisition at an *auto da fé*. He walked slowly, stopping often to kiss the crucifix held to his lips by the attendant confessor, a monk of the Franciscan order, whom it was the convict's privilege to choose for himself to accompany him to the scaffold. He was met there by the executioner, a young man dressed in black who proceeded to bind his naked legs and arms so tightly that they swelled and turned black: a necessary precaution, as this very executioner's father had been killed when struggling with a convict unwilling to die. Veneno made no resistance, but he spoke with supreme contempt of this degraded functionary, saying, " *Mi delito me mata no ese hombre* " (My crime kills me and not this creature). He uttered many pious ejaculations, and his dying cry was, " Viva la Virgen Santisima." The last scene was ghastly in the extreme. While the priest stood by, " a bloated corpulent man more occupied in shading the sun from his face than in his ghostly office," the robber sat with a writhing look of agony, grinding his clenched teeth. The executioner took the lever of the screw in both hands, gathered himself up for a strong muscular effort, drew the iron collar tight while an attendant threw a black handkerchief over the face. A convulsive pressure of the hands and a heaving of the chest were the only visible signs of the passing of the convict's spirit.

"After a pause of a few moments the executioner cautiously peeped under the handkerchief and, after having given another turn of the screw, lifted it off, carefully put it in his pocket and proceeded to light a cigar. The face of the dead man was slightly convulsed, the mouth open, the eye balls turned into their sockets from the wrench. A black bier with two lanterns fixed on staves was now set down before the scaffold. A small table and a dish into which alms were again collected to be paid to the priests who sang masses for his soul was also brought forward. . . . The body remained on the scaffold till after noon. It was then thrown into a scavenger's cart and led by the *pregonero* or common crier beyond the jurisdiction of the city to a square platform called the "mesa del Rey," the king's table, where it was to be quartered and cut up. Here the carcass was hewed and hacked into pieces by the bungling executioner and his assistants."

The condemned cell at the Saladero was a part of the prison chapel in which the Spanish convict spent the last twenty-four hours of life and was a horrible and painfully gruesome hole. The *capilla* is described by de Foresta, who saw it when it was on the eve of abolition. It was of narrow dimensions, damp, dark, windowless and lighted only with one or two small candles burning upon the altar which occupied a large space filling all one wall. In a corner cut off by a black iron railing from the rest of the chapel was a small space fitted with a bed or stone shelf with rings to which the convict's chains were fastened and where he knelt close to the bars to converse with or confess to the ministering priests. The chapel was dimly lighted by a hanging lamp and one or two wax candles. Its walls and floor were damp and it received light and air only through the door. This gruesome den rejoiced in the name *el confortador,* or the " place of comfort."

Another traveller gives the following graphic account of a Spanish execution : —

" At seven we find ourselves in the crowd immediately beneath the prison walls. Large bodies of troops are drawn up on either side of the *plaza* and there is a tolerably large concourse of male spectators present. In a few minutes the mournful cortége appears upon the wall. First comes the executioner, the Spanish Calcraft, a wiry looking fellow, carrying a coil of rope ; next comes a very stout padre armed with a baton, and bawling out prayers at the top of his voice ; he is followed by the convict, who walks on in prison uniform, with his neck

bare and arms pinioned, clasping the cross in his
hands and looking literally in a blue fright; a couple
more priests and two armed sentries complete the
group, who range themselves along the wall, the
criminal in the centre. The terrible scene is long
protracted. The fat padre roars out *Ave Marias*,
exhortations and prayers, waving his baton fran-
tically in the air and making the miserable wretch
repeat after him. He then clasps him in his arms,
and sitting down on chairs opposite each other, they
are covered with a large black pall held by the super-
numerary priests; under this they remain for some
time perfectly motionless, while the poor creature
is unburdening his soul and pouring forth his load
of crimes into the ear of his confessor.

"The nerves of the spectators are strained to an
intense pitch during the awful pause, as is evident
from the oppressive silence which prevails and the
anxious looks directed at the scaffold. At length
the pall is removed and the executioner proceeds to
business. The culprit is made to sit against an upright post to which he is firmly lashed; the *garrote,*
a machine consisting of an iron collar worked back
by a powerful screw and a long lever, is carefully
adjusted round his neck, a small handkerchief
thrown over his face and all is ready. The priest
recommences shouting while the executioner, pre-
paring himself for a mighty effort, suddenly turns
the handle two or three times as quick as light-
ning; the head of the victim drops, the knees and

arms quiver for a few seconds and all is over. Priests and sentries retire, Calcraft peeps under the handkerchief and, whipping it off with a jerk, immediately disappears, leaving the ghastly corpse exposed to open view. It is a sickening and disgusting sight: the face is of a livid hue, the tongue protruding, and shedding saliva on the breast; the bystanders shudder, the troops march off with drums gaily beating and the crowd slowly disperses. I make a rapid sketch of the body and return to the hotel fully satisfied that, were it not for the cruel state of suspense in which the criminal is kept before the execution, the punishment of the *garrote* is far more merciful and expeditious than the less speedy death by hanging in this country."

The profession of hangman does not entitle those who practise it to the very highest honour, although in France in the case of the Sansons it was an hereditary office in which son succeeded father for many generations and the family took considerable pride in their functions. In Spain the *verdugo* is by no means a popular person. De Foresta, the Italian traveller already quoted, tells us that in several towns he saw a person of forbidding aspect who was walking about with a camp stool under his arm and generally shunned. On enquiry he was informed that this was the gentleman who administered the *garrote*. He was strictly forbidden to take a seat at a café or in any place of public resort, hence the camp stool on which he rested himself when tired. No one recognised or addressed to him a single word. De Foresta's comment on this is a story of the French executioner who, when called to Nice to guillotine a criminal, was unable to find anywhere to lay his head. He was turned away from every door, was refused a mouthful of food and was obliged to dine on what he could find at the railway station restaurant, and he spent the night in walking up and down the platform. It may not be generally known that in England the executioner is provided with board and lodging in the gaol where his victim is waiting to be " finished."